Maritime Safety and Security in the Indian Ocean

Maritime Safety and Security in the Indian Ocean

Editors
Vijay Sakhuja
Kapil Narula

National Maritime Foundation

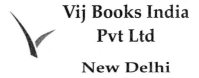

Vij Books India
Pvt Ltd

New Delhi

Published by

Vij Books India Pvt Ltd
(Publishers, Distributors & Importers)
2/19, Ansari Road
Delhi – 110 002
Phones: 91-11-43596460, 91-11-47340674
Fax: 91-11-47340674
e-mail: vijbooks@rediffmail.com
we b: www.vijbooks.com

First Published : 2016

ISBN: 978-93-85563-78-2 (Hardback)

ISBN: 978-93-85563- 79-9 (ebook)

Price in India : ₹ 695/-

Printed and bound in India

Foreword

As the third-largest body of water on Earth, the Indian Ocean is vital for shipping lanes that connect Asia, Oceania and Africa to the rest of the world. The developments in the Indian Ocean affect not only the two billion people living in the countries of the Indian Ocean Region (IOR), but also those in other parts of the globe. Importantly, such interests have manifested over many centuries in the past in various forms including super-power rivalry. The ongoing resurgence of Asia, accompanied by the vigorous economic interactions involving the Asian countries is likely to enhance the salience of the Indian Ocean in the coming decades in a manner that the world has probably never witnessed earlier.

In the context of the 'rise' of Asia, a glance at world history is instructive. It cautions us that the rising level of economic development in our region is not given, and regional prosperity is not pre-ordained; instead, regional countries have to overcome a number of challenges confronting maritime safety and security ranging from regulation of human activities at sea to the impending perils of climate change.

It is encouraging to see that the evolution of the Indian Ocean Rim Association (IORA) from being a nascent grouping of regional countries taking tentative steps to constructively share their economic and cultural diversities to the interconnectedness that the organisation has achieved today. It is also fortuitous that the visionary leadership guiding the IORA realized that economic well-being and prosperity is inextricably linked with good order, safety and security

I am confident that with the momentum that the IORA is gathering, we would be able to overcome the future adversities collectively through identifying appropriate 'regional solutions'. This book is a continuing endeavour and I hope that the views expressed by the participants in this book and the robust process of building consensus through dialogue leads to adoption of specific recommendations which would enhance maritime safety and security in the Indian Ocean.

Admiral DK Joshi,
PVSM, AVSM, YSM, NM, VSM (Retd.)
Chairman
National Maritime Foundation

July 01, 2016

Keynote Address

It is with great pleasure that I join this distinguished group at the IORA Meeting of Experts on Maritime Safety and Security organized by the National Maritime Foundation. I thank all our foreign visitors for their participation in this event and I would like to express appreciation for National Maritime Foundation for the hard work that has gone into organizing this meeting and bringing together the experts and stakeholders gathered here.

The Indian Ocean has facilitated flows of commerce, knowledge as well as culture, and religion across our region since time immemorial. The vast Indian Ocean region is home to nearly 40% of world population. It is almost self-evident that this region holds immense opportunities for the future.

With sustained economic growth in the countries on the littoral of the Indian Ocean, growing global engagement with regional players, as well as the ongoing shift in the global economy's centre of gravity towards Asia, the Indian Ocean has acquired an ever-higher profile. At the same time the region faces challenges flowing from non-traditional threats such as natural disasters, piracy, terrorism, illegal fishing, oil spills and the effects of climate change.

In recent years, the salience of IORA has been growing significantly. This is evident from the fact that the number of States, members of IORA has been growing from 18 in 2011 to 21 in 2015. It is noteworthy that four of five Permanent Members of the UN Security Council are among the six Dialogue Partners of IORA. The number of IORA members and Dialogue Partners is expected to grow further. IORA member countries have shown renewed interest in participating in and launching a number of programmes to coordinate between regional economies in a diverse range of areas and activities. We see IORA as an apex body in the Indian Ocean Region that can respond effectively to the needs of and to enhance individual and collective capacities of Member-States to tackle contemporary challenges of sustainable and balanced economic growth, development and common maritime domain issues.

We in India would like to work with our partners in IORA for a more cooperative and integrated future, and for closer collaboration for the region through the promotion of trade, investment, tourism, infrastructure development, marine science and technology, sustainable fisheries and protection of the marine environment.

The Indian Ocean region from Africa's East coast to West Asia, South Asia and South East Asia and reaching Australia has been in the spotlight of India's foreign policy. Our Prime Minister, Shri Narendra Modi, has succinctly described India's approach in the region as 'SAGAR' – Security and Growth for All in the Region. India seeks to enhance mutual cooperation in our region, to offer our capabilities for the mutual benefit of all in our common oceanic home and assist our neighbours and island states in building their maritime security capabilities. We will all prosper when the seas around us are safe, secure and free for all. We therefore seek collective action and cooperation in the region.

From this perspective, IORA provides an effective multilateral platform that facilitates realization of hitherto untapped opportunities for prosperity, peace and development of the region. India has been working closely with IORA partners to consolidate cooperation under and through this pan-Indian Ocean forum. At the 11th meeting of the IORA Council of Ministers that took place during India's Chairmanship in Bengaluru in November 2011, the members identified six priority areas for cooperation in coming years:

(a) Maritime Safety and Security;

(b) Trade and Investment Facilitation;

(c) Fisheries Management;

(d) Disaster Risk Reduction;

(e) Academic and S&T Cooperation ; and

(f) Tourism Promotion and Cultural Exchanges.

I would submit that experts gathered here for this meeting may look at maritime safety and security issues comprehensively in the IORA context keeping in mind that IORA's primary focus is sustained growth and balanced economic cooperation in the region. This meeting is being hosted in this broader context of IORA cooperation in the six priority areas which include maritime safety and security. The outcomes of discussions here should be focussed, implementable and should factor in both the larger context of IORA and through that perspective focus on maritime safety and security – the theme of this event.

The challenges of maritime safety and security can be best addressed through an inclusive approach. During the deliberations of the 15th bi-annual Committee of Senior Officials (CSOs) in Mauritius in May 2015, India had offered to host such a meeting of experts in maritime safety and security. While IORA includes an IOR Academic Group at Track 1.5 to take forward cooperation in the identified six priority areas, in our view a standalone exchange - bringing together scholars and government officials on a single platform - would help deepen discussions focused on the maritime safety and security issues in the Indian Ocean region. This gathering may be seen against such a backdrop.

I am sure that this meeting would facilitate exchange of ideas, concerns and experiences of IORA Member States. Through this interaction we hope to build greater understanding of the common challenges of maritime safety and security as well as of related areas where we IORA members have synergy, with the aim of enhancing preparedness to effectively respond to multiple challenges.

I wish you all a productive and stimulating discussion. Once again I extend a warm welcome to the participants and thank the National Maritime Foundation for the offer to host this important event.

Ms Sujata Mehta
Secretary (M&ER)
Ministry of External Affairs
Government of India

October 13, 2015

Contents

Appendices

Introduction

The geographical location and embayed disposition of the Indian Ocean Region (IOR) has historically imparted a distinctive character and geo-strategic salience to the region, which continues to the present times. The IOR is also a major source of natural resources particularly hydrocarbons and a busy sea route, and thus essential to the global economy. Nearly half of the world's container shipping, one-third of bulk cargo, and two-thirds of oil shipments are carried onboard ships across the Indian Ocean.

At another level, while the IOR is widely diverse in terms of culture, religion, systems of governance and levels of economic development, its rim countries realize the need for cohesion and cooperation through a pan-IOR grouping. This led to establishment of the Indian Ocean Rim Association for Regional Cooperation (IOR-ARC) in 1995, which was renamed as Indian Ocean Rim Association (IORA) in November 2013 during the 13th meeting of Foreign Ministers at Perth, Australia. The IORA represents a collective will of its member states to enhance economic cooperation for their sustained development and balanced economic growth.

Although 'security' is a relatively recent addition to IORA's agenda, the need to develop cooperative structures in this predominantly maritime-configured region is compelling. The sea-borne economic exchange across the maritime global commons of the IOR is plagued by a variety of non-traditional maritime threats and other security challenges. These range from maritime crimes (piracy, terrorism, drug-trafficking, gun running and human smuggling), natural disasters (tsunamis, cyclones and other natural phenomenon), and resource management issues (unlawful exploitation of living and non-living marine resources, and environment degradation). It is true that many IOR rim countries lack adequate capacity for the safety and security of their maritime interests and have chosen to engage in cooperation, capability-building and 'capacity optimization' of the limited maritime and naval resources to ensure good order at sea in the Indian Ocean. Further, issues such as unresolved maritime boundaries, Illegal Unregulated and Unreported (IUU), and the mushrooming of Private Maritime Security Companies (PMSC) present complex legal challenges, and have further complicated the security environment in the Indian Ocean.

Given the increasing strategic, political and economic significance of the IOR, these issues bear significantly on all stakeholders, both within and beyond the region. In this context, at the 11th IORA Council of Ministers (COM) meeting held in November 2011 at Bengaluru, India, 'Maritime Safety and Security' was among the six identified priority areas for cooperation among the IORA member states. Lately, this has gained greater salience in the deliberations during various meetings and workshops of IORA.

This book is based on the papers presented at the 'IORA Meeting of Experts on Maritime Safety and Security' jointly organized by the Ministry of External Affairs, Government of India and the National Maritime Foundation (NMF) organized from 13- 14 October, 2015 at New Delhi and attempts to understand the approaches of various stakeholders. The meeting examined five thematic areas with the aim to take stock of the collective progress made by IORA member states on maritime safety and security in the region, and also to identify new areas and issues for cooperation.

The first session focused on the regional challenges in maritime safety and security. It attempted to review maritime safety and security challenges and to prioritize them based on identification of 'common denominators'. Issues such as trans-national crime including piracy, terrorism, drug and arms smuggling; Humanitarian Assistance and Disaster Relief (HA/DR) and maritime and aeronautical Search and Rescue (SAR); Illegal, Unreported and Unregulated (IUU) fishing and resource management for sustainable development were addressed.

The second session addressed the cooperative organisational structures in the IOR. Maritime safety and security structures and current programmes of member states, including inter-state arrangements were discussed. The way ahead for harmonization of existing regional / sub-regional groupings and agreements, and developing a pan-IOR web of functional arrangements including linking of IORA and IONS was deliberated. The importance of domain awareness, information-sharing mechanism, and designation of nodal agencies/ Point of Contact (PoC) for collation and dissemination for data management was emphasized. The feasibility of the Indian Ocean Dialogue (IOD) as a mechanism for undertaking discussions was also explored.

Session three dealt with an inclusive approach to maritime safety and security. The role of extra regional stakeholders/Dialogue Partners/ organisations such as ASEAN and ARF was deliberated. Norms for extra-regional stakeholders *inter alia* for freedom of navigation, and maritime capacity building and security assistance were considered. The role of private/ commercial stakeholders and Corporate Social Responsibility (CSR) in enhancing maritime safety and security was also explored.

Legal Frameworks were explored in session four. The members unanimously agreed that regional dispute resolutions mechanisms should be undertaken within the framework of international law. It emerged that the efforts must be taken to build legal capacity of member states and an IORA Legal Expert Working Group on maritime safety and security could contribute to this goal.

The last session on capability building and capacity optimization included a discussion on national maritime safety and security institutions/ agencies, their mandates and capacities. The requirement of technical/ hardware, technology sharing, training and exercises as well as providing security assistance to countries also emerged as key points for deliberations.

This book provides a comprehensive view of the perspectives of IORA stakeholder's and while highlighting the regional challenges, presents solutions to enhance maritime security and security in the region. We hope that it will go a long way in understanding and enhancing maritime safety and security in the Indian Ocean.

– Vijay Sakhuja

– Kapil Narula

Maritime Safety and Security Challenges: A Singaporean Perspective

Koh Swee Lean Collin

Abstract

The Indian Ocean is important to Singapore's national interests given the island city-state's geostrategic location. Towards the end of securing and promoting these interests in the Indian Ocean, Singapore has not only participated in regional institutions but also serves a modest "security provider" role as seen in its deployment of naval forces to join multinational counter-piracy operations off Somalia. However, because of the limitations of Singapore's resource capacity, it becomes imperative to advocate an inclusive approach towards addressing the myriad of maritime safety and security challenges in the Indian Ocean. This includes focusing on building the capacities of the countries bordering the Indian Ocean, as well as careful involvement of extra-regional powers which bring forth niche capabilities.

Introduction

Southeast Asia sits at the confluence between the Indian Ocean and the Pacific Ocean. Singapore's geostrategic location is peculiar in this regard. Even though its seaboard barely faces the expanse of the eastern rim of the Indian Ocean, given its dependence on access to the international Sea Lines of Communications (SLOCs) for national survival and prosperity, the small island city-state is exposed to maritime safety and security developments in the Indian Ocean Region (IOR). Most crucially, Singapore sits astride the Malacca Strait – one of the world's most crucial waterways and an important chokepoint – that connects the two oceans. This geostrategic position Singapore finds itself in thus makes this island city-state one of the key player. This is especially so when one takes into account two recent major developments.

1

The first concerns the rising salience of the IOR as part of the broader Asian region's strategic calculus. Chiefly of all, the Indian Ocean Rim Association (IORA) has steadily gathered pace to build institutional processes amongst its member states. Second, is the increasing geopolitical focus on the IOR by different actors. The recently revised maritime strategy released by Washington couched its strategic approach within the "Indo-Asia-Pacific" construct, thus reflecting its cognizance of the rising role played by IOR.[1] This also coincides with China's increasing forays into the IOR, including economic and military outreaches to the rim countries. Japan has also become a recent player in the IOR, in part because of its continued reliance on energy imports from the region but also due to its ongoing rivalry with China.

Much has been written about major powers' perspectives on the IOR. So this chapter seeks to espouse the small state's perspectives of Singapore. Not unlike the major powers, Singapore also possesses vested interests in the IOR. Certainly Singapore does not have such grand scheme of ideas for the IOR compared to the major powers, but nonetheless, it remains exposed to variable developments taking place in the region. In upholding its national interests, Singapore necessarily has to be cognizant of the maritime safety and security challenges in the IOR. But "challenges" ought to transcend just "threats" or "risks" to those interests. It ought to be seen in a holistic manner. When one considers "challenges", the idea of vulnerability ought to be examined. So what is vulnerability? Seen holistically, vulnerability is a function of threats and the ability to mitigate those threats. There is one more catch to that: the potential consequences that stem from the collective imperative to mitigate those threats.

With this analytical framework in mind, this chapter first briefly looks at the threats to Singapore's interests in the IOR. It then goes on to look at how Singapore mitigates those threats. The chapter concludes with final thoughts on the potential consequences of mitigating maritime safety and security threats.

Threats: The First Layer of Analysis

Much has been discussed about the diverse range of maritime safety and security threats to the IOR.[2] Rather like the Western Pacific rim which has traditionally been Singapore's primary focus, the IOR is geographically broad and heterogeneous, comprising a diverse number of countries with differing national contexts and circumstances, ranging from political, economic, sociocultural and military.[3] This means differing and at times conflictual national interests and this thereby shape how one views those threats. But the point to note is that the types of threats in the Western Pacific rim bear some differences with those in the IOR. Many of the most acute maritime flashpoints are located in the former, for example the East and South China Seas disputes. By contrast, the IOR has been relatively peaceful and stable in this regard. India for example resolved the maritime boundary dispute via international arbitration with Bangladesh.

Despite these contextual differences, there are similarities where threat perceptions are concerned. First of all, there ought to be virtual agreement amongst the IOR countries that the SLOCs passing through the region are of utmost importance to not just national survival and prosperity, but also the regional and international well-being at large. This naturally implies common concerns about safety and security to shipping from a myriad of hazards, for example piracy and armed robbery against ships. The more recent international reports showed that piracy attacks have been declining off the Horn of Africa, and the focus of attention has been shifting towards East Asian waters such as the Malacca Strait and South China Sea where there have been resurgent incidents.[4] But transnational crimes remain a major concern, especially the case of the Rohingya refugees and their seaborne voyages even though the scale of this problem certainly pales in comparison to that observed in the Mediterranean. In more recent times, the threat posed by religious extremism and militancy, especially that posed by the Islamic State, shows that unconventional security threats know no boundaries. It may just be a matter of time that religious extremism and militancy broadens into the maritime domain, posing new dangers to SLOC security.[5]

These man-made threats aside, the second type of threat that sees virtual agreement amongst IOR countries are natural calamities. The Indian Ocean earthquake and tsunami in December 2004 showed that the surrounding rim countries can be affected in various degrees. In more recent years, new contingencies emerged. In particular, one notes the missing Malaysia Airlines flight MH 370 in March 2014 and the sustained duration of search-and-locate operations involving countries across the Indo-Asia-Pacific. It exemplifies the rising salience of aeronautical and maritime contingencies in the region, not least further reinforced by the loss of Air Asia flight QZ 8501 in late December the same year. These unconventional security threats are shown to be multi-faceted, trans-boundary in nature and that no one nation-state can single-handedly deal with them alone. What happens in the IOR has spillover effects on the surrounding sub-regions, Southeast Asia included. As such, cooperation becomes necessary in order to mitigate those threats.

Mitigation: The Second Layer of Analysis

Indeed, Singapore as a small country which is heavily dependent on maritime trade finds itself particularly sensitive to the surrounding, evolving security landscape. As a self-help measure, which is in line with its long-upheld security policy of maintaining its relevance to the international community[6], Singapore has become more involved in international security operations in the IOR, most notably for example counter-piracy missions as part of CTF151 in the Gulf of Aden (Operation Blue Sapphire) since 2009. The strategic rationale for devoting manpower and resources to such far-flung regions is no less different from many other East Asian countries which have legitimate security stakes in the IOR, chiefly of all energy-related. It is likely that Singapore will continue to devote attention to the IOR through limited military deployments and provision of niche capabilities, such as the recently promulgated Regional Humanitarian Assistance and Disaster Relief Coordination Centre (RHCC), based alongside the Information Fusion Centre in Changi Naval Base.

However, it is clear that due to its size, geostrategic position and resource constraints it becomes imperative for Singapore to seek collective solutions with other nation-states to address those maritime safety and security threats. This thus poses the third, less spoken-of aspect of maritime safety and security challenge if, again, one looks beyond threats to national maritime interests but also the ability of relevant stakeholders in mitigating those vulnerabilities. In this connection, one needs to adopt a realistic outlook on the IOR's ability to mitigate those maritime safety and security threats. The IOR is a much wider geographical region comprising littoral states with not just differing national contexts and circumstances but also disparities in capabilities and capacities. Only a number of IOR countries possess the requisite capabilities to respond to major maritime safety and security threats. For instance, India and Singapore demonstrated their sealift capabilities following the tsunami in 2004, by contributing to surrounding IOR neighbours.[7] Australia and India were at the forefront of the search-and-locate missions for MH370, since they possess the requisite long-range maritime patrol and surveillance capabilities to cover such vast area as the southern Indian Ocean.[8] Inevitably, the better-endowed IOR countries are relied upon to provide more "public security goods", Singapore being one of them. But clearly also, depending on such a small handful of these better-endowed countries is not sufficient. The existing capabilities and capacities are just spread too thinly across the region.

In the age of shrinking defence dollars and the need to cope with such a diverse range of maritime safety and security threats, a more sustainable long-term solution will be for every littoral state in the IOR to step up its national capacities. Better-endowed IOR countries can assist in such capacity-building processes. For example, Singapore-based Regional Cooperation Agreement on Combating Piracy and Armed Robbery against Ships in Asia (Re CAAP) information sharing centre helped East African countries build information-sharing centres to deal with piracy incidents.[9] India has traditionally helped the smaller littoral states in the IOR build their national capacities, for example helping Seychelles build coastal surveillance radar infrastructure[10] or supplying offshore patrol vessels to the Maldives, Mauritius and Sri Lanka. As a way to help stem the tide of refugee vessels heading towards Australian shores, Canberra also donated patrol craft to Colombo in 2014.[11] Such financial and technical assistance will continue, but contingent on the assisting countries' capacities as well as the recipient countries' ability to absorb such assistance. Because of the diverse nature of the IOR, such capacity-building process inevitably has to take time. In the interim, the better-endowed IOR countries need to fill the void in providing those critical "public security goods". However, the envisaged end-goal ought to be more efficient pooling and utilization of resources in order to effectively deal with the threats across the entire geographical expanse of the IOR.

Concurrently, there is a need to start promoting institutionalized forms of cooperation so that collective solutions become a habit instead of ad-hoc processes. This dual-tracked approach does not refer to just the military, but a wide range of non-military, civilian agencies in what can be deemed a "whole of government" approach. While the militaries continue to serve as a reliable bulwark in providing timely and substantial response to various security challenges, it is no longer a tenable prospect to overlook the useful roles played by other non-military or non-state entities such as civilian maritime law enforcement agencies. Therefore, it becomes necessary to bring these diverse entities together, leverage on one another's strengths and promote a habit of cooperation. This ought to take place at both national and regional levels. International agencies dealing with maritime-related affairs, for example the International Maritime Organization, can play crucial roles in capacity-building. But again, one needs to harp on the importance of national capacity-building efforts. One potential area of concern is that governments may not be willing to cooperate because of their cognizance of lack of capacities which they bring to the table. While it can be assumed that given the financial and technical abilities, each country may strive to develop a balanced range of capabilities, it may help to focus on niche areas for national capacity-building to minimize duplication or overlapping of efforts.

Final Layer of Analysis: Potential Consequences of Mitigating Threats

It would, however, be simplistic to think of challenges in the IOR maritime domain solely as a function of threats and mitigation. In the process of mitigating those threats, there are bound to be friction and disagreement on how best to collectively address those issues. Taking other contemporary regional institutions, such as the Association of Southeast Asian Nations (ASEAN) and the European Union (EU) for example, intra-bloc dissent is not a unique problem. This is especially the case when individual member states may have their own overarching national interests that can precede those of the organization as a whole. Their own national contexts and circumstances shape those interests, including how and in what way extra-regional parties can play a role.

This problem is certainly replicated in IORA, especially given its heterogeneity of membership. It does not mean that having a common platform for cooperation dispels all the potential for friction and discord. ASEAN's common platform has been regional architecture-building via the ASEAN way for example. In the case of IORA, the Blue Economy concept which calls for sustainable and shared development in the maritime domain as its core theme constitutes one such platform. It allows IOR countries to come together, conceive common challenges and find collective ways to address those challenges. But clearly, IORA member states are not the only stakeholders despite their geographical positions. Other extra-regional powers have legitimate interests as well. Foremost of all has been to ensure continuous, uninterrupted access to energy supplies from the Middle East and Africa. Seaborne transport of energy invariably has to pass through the Indian Ocean before reaching, say, the Northeast Asian economic powerhouses such as China, Japan and South Korea. These countries can claim legitimate stakes in the IOR maritime safety and security. It is also primarily because of these interests related to SLOC security that they have deployed naval forces to fight piracy off the Horn of Africa since 2008.

Some of these extra-regional stakeholders may have national agendas that fit with what the IOR countries may have. The Blue Economy is one such example. Possessing variable capacities that others can possibly tap on, these extra-regional stakeholders can be encouraged to play a constructive role in mitigating IOR maritime safety and security threats. In fact, a number of these countries are already involved to some degree. For example, other than assisting in the construction of vital port and shipping infrastructure, in no small part to help ameliorate China's own energy insecurity,[12] Beijing is also helping with maritime safety and security building efforts as part of bilateral engagements with individual IOR countries. But at the same time, China's involvement in the IOR is not without controversy. China's expanding naval footprints in the region, including the deployment of submarines, has become a matter of concern for New Delhi,[13] with whom Beijing has its own set of enduring bilateral problems which are yet to be resolved. It becomes inevitable that China's forays into the IOR may be viewed with suspicion. Yet India cannot possibly wish China away, especially not when China's entry has been welcomed by countries such as the Maldives and Sri Lanka, if not all other IOR countries.[14]

Therefore, what it means is that in the process of extra-regional involvement in the IOR there is bound to be "strategic friction" as a result of contradicting or conflictual interests. This friction that comes along with geopolitical sensitivities, if not managed properly may lead to the unintended consequences of interstate rivalries and conflict. In this regard, given diverse regional perceptions towards extra-regional involvement in the IOR, inclusivity becomes essential. To bring in extra-regional powers to work with IOR countries, harness their capacities and to minimize the likelihood of "strategic friction" it is necessary to build multilateral institutional mechanisms. These platforms can serve as a vehicle for practical maritime safety and security cooperation as well as build confidence. IORA thus plays this pivotal role. IORA may be young compared to other comparable regional organizations such as ASEAN. Nonetheless, it is believed that with a deliberate, long-term, inclusive and phased "building block" roadmap that takes into account contemporary realities while seeking to address them through sustained collective efforts from all member states and external stakeholders, it is possible to overcome maritime safety and security challenges in the IOR.

Conclusion

This chapter essentially captures the Singaporean perspective of IOR maritime safety and security challenges. It is necessary to regard this challenge in a holistic manner, by looking at them in terms of threats, the ability to mitigate those threats and not to forget taking into consideration the potential consequences. The IOR is a diverse, heterogeneous and complex region to start with. Common threats originate from unconventional sources which have strategic ramifications for the region as a whole, yet at the same time each IOR country possesses its own national agenda shaped by unique threat perceptions and varying resource capacities. In the long term, it is argued here, it is necessary for all IOR countries to level up in terms of capabilities and capacities so as to efficiently pool resources to cope with the threats. This challenge is one that will necessarily take time to overcome, given the anticipated enormous amount of resources to fulfill existing capacity shortfalls. At the same time, it is necessary to rely on the small handful of better-endowed IOR countries. But clearly this is just an interim solution. In the foreseeable longer term, extra-regional involvement is to be expected as an enduring fixture in the IOR. These extra-regional stakeholders bring with them their own legitimate security interests in the IOR and also, their capabilities to offer to the region. It will be a matter of pragmatism to tap on their capacities, yet at the same time cognizant of the geopolitical sensitivities as a result of interstate differences. This strategic friction can only be overcome by inclusivity in the region, while promoting institution-building focusing on strengthening the IORA as the key process that can propel the IOR forward. This can only be done in an incremental manner, through a "building block" approach that every IOR country can agree on. The Blue Economy, which calls for sustainable and shared development in the maritime dimension, constitutes a common platform to bring together the diverse national interests of IOR countries and extra-regional stakeholders.

Notes

1 United States Navy, A Cooperative Strategy for 21st Century Seapower, March 2015. Available at: http://www.navy.mil/local/maritime/150227-CS21R-Final.pdf (accessed on 28 October 2015)

2 Read for example, Aditi Chatterjee, "Non-traditional Maritime Security Threats in the Indian Ocean Region," Maritime Affairs: Journal of the National Maritime Foundation of India, 2014, pp. 1-19; and Lee Cordner, "Maritime security in the Indian Ocean region: Compelling and convergent agendas," Australian Journal of Maritime and Ocean Affairs, Vol. 2, No. 1 (2010), pp. 16-27.

3 Cordner, "Maritime security in the Indian Ocean region," p. 16.

4 The number of piracy attacks off Somalia fell further to 12 in 2014 from 20 in 2013, significantly lower than the 78 incidents reported in 2007. Even though compared to 142 incidents reported in 2013, the number of incidents which took place in the South China Sea saw a decrease to 93 in 2014, this figure remains high. A total of 81 incidents in the Straits of Malacca and Singapore were registered. It needs pointing out that approximately 40% of the attacks worldwide were reported to have occurred or to have been attempted in territorial waters, largely due to an increase in armed robbery activity in the Strait of Malacca. Reports on Acts of Piracy and Armed Robbery against Ships: Annual Report – 2014, MSC.4/Circ.219/Rev.1 (London: International Maritime Organization, 28 April 2015), p. 2.

5 The Islamic State in July 2015 claimed to have attacked a moored Egyptian coastguard patrol vessel in the Mediterranean Sea near the Sinai Peninsula, using a guidedmissile. Savahna Nightingale, "Islamic State militants claim Egypt coastguard attack," IHS Maritime 360, 21 July 2015. Available at: http://www.ihsmaritime360.com/article/18696/islamic-state-militants-claim-egypt-coastguard-attack (accessed on 29 October 2015)

6 Speech by Senior Minister Professor S Jayakumar at the S Rajaratnam Lecture at Shangri-La Hotel on Wednesday 19 May 2010, Ministry of Foreign Affairs, Singapore.

7 Prior to the disaster, within the IOR only these countries possess large amphibious landing vessels capable of undertaking major sealift operations in support of humanitarian assistance and disaster relief (HA/DR) missions: Australia, India and Singapore. The Indonesian Navy had the 122m landing platform docks on order from South Korea and not delivered when disaster struck. It was only following the tsunami that Jakarta decided to ramp up HA/DR capabilities, including a follow-on purchase of more of the LPDs. Thailand also followed suit years later with the purchase of a single LPD from Singapore, almost similar to the ones the latter deployed in the aftermath of the tsunami

to Aceh.

8   China possesses no equivalent to the US Navy's P-3 Orion or P-8 Poseidon long-range MPA, thus deployed its Russian-built Il-76 strategic airlifter to conduct visual SAL operations in the southern Indian Ocean. But besides airborne endurance, other requisite capabilities are needed to precisely locate and identify small debris or large objects of the airplane floating on the rough seas, such as high-definition surface search radars and electro-optical sensors for day and night, all-weather use. Such capabilities cannot be found on a typical strategic airlifter. Such well-equipped long-range MPAs find service only with Australia, India and New Zealand in the vicinity.

9   ReCAAP ISC's Contribution to the Djibouti Code of Conduct (Singapore: Regional Cooperation Agreement on Combating Piracy and Armed Robbery against Ships in Asia Information Sharing Centre (ISC), n.d.), available at: http://www.recaap.org/LinkClick.aspx?fileticket=sf_ Tcgby0IY%3D&tabid=93&mid=542 (accessed on 20 October 2015)

10   "India begins infrastructure work on Assumption Island of Seychelles," *Sarkaritel*, 27 August 2015.

11   The first ex-Australian Customs and Border Protection Vessel (ACV) of the Bay class was transferred to Sri Lanka in April 2014, followed by the second one about two months later. "Australian Bay class Patrol Vessel to Complement Sri Lankan Navy," *Sri Lankan Government News*, 1 April 2014; "Australian Customs and Border Protection Service Marks Gifting of 2nd Bay class Patrol Boat," *Australian Government News*, 3 June 2014.

12   Read for instance, Marc Lanteigne, "China's Maritime Security and the "Malacca Dilemma"," *Asian Security*, Vol. 4, No. 2 (2008), pp. 143-161.

13   "Navy monitoring Chinese activity in Indian Ocean: Navy Chief," *Press Trust of India*, 25 September 2014.

14   For example, the Maldives and Sri Lanka are supportive of Beijing's 21st entury Maritime Silk Road Initiative and its outreach to the IOR littoral states. "Sri Lanka supports China's initiative of a 21st Century Maritime Silk Route," *Daily News (Sri Lanka)*, 22 February 2014; "Maldives to officially join China's maritime silk route policy," *Xinhua News Agency*, 16 December 2014. Even if one discounts these initiatives, the fact that Pakistan has an enduring close strategic partnership with China, especially allowing Beijing access to the port in Gwadar, gives Beijing reason to remain engaged in the IOR in order to safeguard its national interests, especially those related to energy security.

Maritime Safety and Security Challenges: A Sri Lankan Perspective

Bhagya Senaratne

Abstract

Island countries of the Indian Ocean Region face many maritime security challenges, such as piracy, trafficking of illicit drugs and people, environmental concerns, border security etc. Straddled centrally in the region, Sri Lanka has issues unique to itself like its close proximity to the Sea Lanes of Communication, the nuclear power status of its South Asian neighbours, environmental concerns, illegal fishing in its EEZ, inundation of the coastal region etc. This chapter encapsulates the challenges faced by Sri Lanka in the past and present. It also highlights some of the maritime security and safety challenges it can face in the future. The chapter highlights some of the measures which the government has also already taken and provides insight into actions it can take in the future independently and along with other countries in the region to mitigate these issues.

Introduction

Since time immemorial the Indian Ocean, stretching from the Strait of Hormuz to the Strait of Malacca and the Strait of Mandeb to the Lombok Strait, has been an important location in the strategic calculations of the great powers of the world. This is primarily due to the economic impact of the Indian Ocean in the east-west maritime trade. The Indian Ocean covers twenty percent of the earth and is ranked as the third largest water coverage in the world. However, over the last decade, the Indian Ocean Region (IOR) has emerged as a focus of international concern, not merely because of its great strategic salience but also due to the enormous market potential. Due to this the IOR is increasingly becoming a global hotspot in both regional and international dialogue. Therefore, this is without a doubt an important region for the world in the future years.

It is through this region that half of the world's container traffic passes and whose ports handle approximately thirty percent of world trade thus becoming the "economic highway of the world".[1] "...66% of oil shipments so vital for India, Japan and China... and 33% of the world's bulk cargo" passes through these waters.[2] Continental Shelves cover approximately forty two percent of the Indian Ocean which is said to be rich in minerals such as Tin, Gold, Uranium, Cobalt, Nickel, Aluminium and Cadmium. Its global significance is further reiterated as forty out of fifty four types of raw materials used by U.S. industries are sourced from the Indian Ocean and it possesses some of the world's largest fishing grounds, providing approximately fifteen percent of the world's total fish catch (approximately 9 million tons per annum). Furthermore, fifty five percent of the Earth's known oil reserves are present in the Indian Ocean and forty percent of the world's natural gas reserves are in the Indian Ocean littoral states.[3] These facts related primarily to the economy, influences the importance which this region retains on global politics.

Maritime Safety and Security Challenges

Unlike the other states of this region, Sri Lanka is located strategically as an island in the centre of the IOR. Hambantota[4], near Sri Lanka's southernmost point is "close to the world's main shipping lanes where more than thirty thousand vessels per year transport fuel and raw material from the Middle East to East Asia".[5] And due to the convenient positioning, "Sri Lanka has not been immune from these strategic calculations and speculations".[6] Therefore, maritime security and safety lie at the heart of Sri Lankan interests in the region and her national security policies. The significance it plays in Sri Lanka's interests can be identified by statements made by Sri Lankan Diplomats such as Sri Lanka's former High Commissioner to India, Prasad Kariyawasam, who stated "... [Sri Lanka] will always act in a manner that contributes to strategic stability in the region. This also serves our national interest of securing enhanced maritime security in and around the Indian Ocean as well as ensuring peace in the region".[7] Therefore, whilst projecting and promoting itself as a "strategic node of global maritime commerce" Sri Lanka also has to be mindful of its security implications in being so closely located to the world's busiest shipping routes which transports "one half of the world's container traffic".[8]

In this context, it is also worth noting that both regional and extra-regional powers such as India, China and the United States of America have shown an increasing interest towards the Indian Ocean and have towards this end, engineered grand strategies such as the Indian Ocean Strategy, the Maritime Silk Route initiative and the New Silk Road respectively. In addition to the benefits derived from interacting with the IOR littorals, all three nations have also identified Sri Lanka, with its strategic location as an ideal focal point to implement its policies and objectives.

Globalisation largely relies on sea lanes and in this context the Indian Ocean sea lanes are of critical importance to trade and energy security. This is because the region "accounts for seventy percent of the traffic of petroleum products for the entire world".[9] Oil and gas laden ships travel from the Persian Gulf, transit around Sri Lanka into the waters of South China Sea, whilst reciprocal traffic carrying finished goods from China, Japan, Korea and Taiwan moves the other way. During this long voyage, ships run the risk of encountering piracy, maritime terrorism and inter-state conflict. And this worries many nations whose economies are dependent on trade and energy. Due to this reason the Sri Lankan defence authorities have identified that "...the energy security of many nations depends on the Indian Ocean, as the fuel requirements of many industrialising nations are met through the energy resources transported through it. For all these reasons and more, the Indian Ocean's importance in the global context is very great".[10]

At this juncture Sri Lanka can take the lead in providing and ensuring maritime security. As maritime security is driven by market forces, Sri Lanka with its capable navy can assist in protecting ships passing through the Sea Lines of Communications (SLOCs) acting as a neutral figure in providing equal protection to everyone. This enables the reduction of extra-regional powers in and around the island, thus reducing the tension caused to its immediate neighbours, such as India. Further, keeping its non-aligned policy at the core, Sri Lanka can also assist in enhancing global safety by being the chief neutral security point in the IOR by monitoring piracy threats and all the naval vessels that transit the region. Therefore, should the need arise Sri Lanka should take the precedence in calling for action. Not only would this include monitoring of surface ships, but also activities of all submarines, in order for them not to infringe on the territorial integrity of Sri Lanka as well as the region at large. And here, the

1971 Declaration of the Indian Ocean as a Zone of Peace becomes relevant and important. Therefore it will be very useful and beneficial for the region if the United Nations arrives at a consensus for its implementation.

In addition to the central geographical positioning, Sri Lanka's deep depths close to the shore in Hambantota where there is a manmade harbour and the deep natural harbour in Trincomalee[11] makes it easily accessible by even Triple E ships. With its central location, Sri Lanka needs to assert this stance and project itself as an entrepôt for goods transiting to both the east and the west, similar to the early 1400s when the Chinese utilised ancient Ceylon as an entrepôt between China and the Middle East.[12] Sri Lanka needs to be assertive and play a proactive role in the region's trade dynamics. Doing this will enable Sri Lanka to safeguard its maritime security and to mitigate any challenges. It should also be noted that seventy percent of the Indian cargo transships through the Colombo Port. Therefore, it is wise for both regional economies that want access to global trade and vice versa to utilise Sri Lanka in their trading endeavours as it is not only a central location but a low cost destination with access to a large number of destinations due to its non-aligned status. And to this end, the future development plans of the Colombo Port, by way of the on-going Colombo Port Expansion Project will be beneficial in reaching potential markets.

Earlier on in 2015, Prime Minister Modi expressed this capability and the potential of enhancement of economic activities in the Indian Ocean during his address to the Sri Lankan Parliament when he stated that "Connecting this vast region by land and sea, our two countries can become engines of regional prosperity. We have made good progress today. Let us get together to harness the vast potential of the Ocean Economy".[13] This emphasises that there is continued potential for Sri Lanka to harness and work alongside other regional entities in safeguarding its economic security interests in this region.

As the first line of defence in the country Sri Lanka Navy's primary role is to ensure sea control and denial to enemy by conducting day and night surveillance at sea to prevent warlike material coming into the country and preventing illicit poaching in the Exclusive Economic Zone (EEZ).[14] In 1998 the Sri Lanka Coast Guard (SLCG) was established to ensure safety and security of Sri Lanka's coastal areas, territorial waters and maritime zones together with the Sri Lanka Navy. This enables Sri Lanka to monitor the vessels entering and exiting its shores and exercise control over it.[15] Since its establishment in 1806 the Department of Sri Lanka Customs assists in this endeavour by collecting revenue, enforcing law and overseeing activities at both the airport and the Colombo Port[16,17]. This double monitoring of Sri Lanka's borders and ports enables the country to reduce transnational crimes and scrutinise such activities.

Due to the vastness of the Indian Ocean it becomes increasingly difficult for it to be monitored. Therefore similar to the high seas being open and easily accessible for economic purposes, it is also utilised for less ethical activities. Due to the centrality of its location, Sri Lanka continues to be utilised as a transit point for drug smuggling from the 'Golden Triangle' and the 'Golden Crescent'. "Heroin is routed via Sri Lanka from Pakistan or India on a big scale by containers and mechanized fishing craft".[18] Trafficking of arms via sea routes is one of the safest means of transferring arms and ammunition which leads to conflicts and disputes that can destabilise a country as well as an entire region. Often drug and arms trafficking work hand-in-hand and is currently one of the pressing security issues faced by Sri Lanka.

Since 2007, maritime piracy has become a major security threat to global commercial trade. Piracy in the high seas affects the region in both the east and west with threats in the Strait of Malacca and the Strait of Bab-el-Mandeb respectively. The threat from the Somali pirates in the west recently came close to the Maldives, thus showcasing the reach and the sophistication of these illegal groups. The demarcated High Risk Area (HRA) closer to Sri Lanka threatens Sri Lanka's security and it affects maritime trade and commerce and it could pose a serious problem to the SLOC in the future. Therefore not only will maritime piracy affect Sri Lanka's borders, it will also severely threaten the country's economic security as well.

Sri Lanka Navy and Sri Lanka Coast Guard have to a larger extent managed to curtail Sri Lankans being smuggled to developed countries for better economic opportunities. In the past, organised groups connected to the LTTE lured people seeking better economic opportunities via its illegal operations. In this case, though human trafficking does not directly affect the country's border security, it indirectly affects the country. However, Sri Lanka is currently facing the challenge of combating the country being utilised as a transit hub to smuggle people to other countries. Therefore, with the changing nature of global politics, Sri Lanka will have to strengthen its security measures to continue safeguarding its shores from being used for such illegal activities.

Sri Lanka has taken stringent measures such as reinforcing its law enforcement agencies, for instance the Sri Lanka Police with the Narcotics Bureau to curtail the spread of illicit drugs in the country. Along with the trade of illicit drugs other illegal activities such as money laundering become widespread not only within a single country, but in the entire region. In this light the Indian Ocean littorals have to step up efforts to safeguard its coastal belt and the Sri Lanka Coast Guard can contribute enormously to this effort. It must be noted that seas and coastlines are the areas where most trade is conducted and along which most humanity lives.[19] Owing to this it can be foreseen that transnational crimes will continue to be on the rise.

Supported by the U.S. Government, the Colombo Mega Port Programme assists in keeping a check on potential radioactive devices and equipment entering the country. The principal objective of this programme is to reduce the risk of illicit trafficking of Special Nuclear Materials (SNM) and other radioactive isotopes that might be used in Weapons of Mass Destruction (WMD) or Radiological Dispersal Device (RDD) before they reach the borders of the United States. To this end the U.S. has decided to direct all their imports through mega ports located worldwide which while is economically advantageous to Sri Lanka is also a cause for concern as there is a risk of these radioactive isotopes entering the island's shores.

Another border related security challenge faced by Sri Lanka is the protection of its maritime resources. Illegal fishing by South Indian fisherman, in Sri Lankan waters since the defeat of terrorism is a serious concern for the country's resources as these activities are conducted on a large scale and advertently affects the livelihood of the local fisher folk. The other threat to border security is that illegal fishing also leads to collaboration with equally damaging illegal activities such as trafficking of drugs etc. Taking into consideration the impending and future maritime security threats facing the country, it is pertinent to strengthen and expand the responsibilities of both the Navy and the Coast Guard. The two agencies have the enormous task of ensuring security from the borders to the EEZ to the seas around the nation. Thus, expanding and securing more naval assets that enable the navy to patrol the blue waters will be advantageous as the Indian Ocean is set to be the dominant region in this century.

Due to the expanse of the ocean and availability of marine resources, fishing is another factor that plays an important role in the IOR. Illegal, Unreported and Unregulated (IUU) fishing by small and large scale businesses tend to threaten the marine resources and ecosystems mainly due to the lack of regulation or the inability to monitor certain illegal fishing activities. Sri Lankan waters are abundant with marine resources which provide a great source of income to the fisher folk of the island. However, due to the wealth of fishing resources, the EEZ is being threatened by IUU activities around the island. Further, bottom trawling, use of illegal fishing nets, and the use of explosives and poison have become both a security and safety threat to Sri Lanka. To this end, Sri Lanka Navy faces a huge challenge in safeguarding the waters and resources from illegal fishing activities.

Increasing global temperatures are affecting islands and their coastlines. As a result the Sri Lankan coastline too is affected due to changes in the global climatic conditions with predictions indicating that a significant proportion of the island's coastline would be underwater. A projected rise in sea level of between 0.2m - 0.6m would see the inundation of the coastal regions of Negombo, Colombo, Galle etc.[20] However studies have revealed that it would take an 8m rise of sea level for the submergence of the island's coastal region.

The Sethusamudram Shipping Canal Project is another specific challenge to not only Sri Lanka's economy but also to its environment. India is keen on implementing this project as it "does not have a continuous navigable route"[21] and this project would "enable ships to avoid circumnavigating Sri Lanka".[22] However as much as this canal will impact on the commercial status of Colombo, it will also threaten the environment and marine resources in the Palk Strait. The canal will significantly affect the livelihood of the fishermen and the risk arising from possible oil spills may affect the fragile marine environment in the region.

There are various other security threats to the region such as the nuclear capability of two of the major powers of South Asia. The small states in the region that neither possesses such capabilities nor has access to this technology is at an increasing security risk. Thus the nuclear weapons pose a security threat to the national security as well as the human security of these small states that are non-nuclear weapon states. According to Thomas P. M. Barnett, "No ocean is in need of strategic stability more than the Indian Ocean, which is arguably the most nuclearised of the seven seas."[23] Not only does the region possess its own nuclear giants, it also sees "nuclear powers whose navies ply this ocean such as the United States, the United Kingdom, France, Russia, China, India, Pakistan, and Israel".[24] Further India's nuclear power reactors in Kalpakkam near Chennai, Koodankulam and "the experimental establishments in Kerala"[25] pose a serious threat to Sri Lanka as any accident would directly affect the island due to its close proximity.

Conclusion

Sri Lanka, straddled conveniently in the great Indian Ocean Region is a leader in advancing cooperation in South Asia. And, it is important for the future of the region that small states such as Sri Lanka develop and partake in its security and development. Gradually increasing international shipping traffic will increase the inflow of not only ships but men and material amplifying the potential security hazards from overseas. Therefore Sri Lanka needs to ensure a secure environment for the users for unfettered development of trade and commerce. Recognising these security implications, in 2008 Sri Lanka expressed the need to adopt a National Strategy for Maritime Security of Sri Lanka.[26] Therefore, it can be assessed that it is time for the island to adopt a National Strategy for Maritime Security incorporating the aforementioned salient points, neutrality and the non-aligned stance taken in its foreign policy.

Due to the emerging strategic environment in the IOR, Sri Lanka has an enormous obligation to prevent transnational crimes, ensure the safe passage of merchant ships and to prevent terrorist activities in the EEZ and beyond. As global economies develop, the greatest maritime challenge posed to the island would be the safety and surveillance of the SLOC. With a large mass of water towards the southern end of the country, Sri Lanka is obliged to enhance its capacity and capability in Search and Rescue Operations (SAR). It needs to optimise itself to the level where it can lead such operations in the region along with other friendly nations.

Further according to Kaplan "...the future of military activity will be maritime in nature as military activity tends to follow trade and economic activity".[27] If Sri Lanka does not revamp its security measures in the IOR, it will feature prominently in these military activities if and when it does occur. After all it is forecasted that the IOR will be at the centre of global politics. Sharing intelligence via available mechanisms will be an added advantage to the countries of this region as it can mitigate unprecedented maritime threats to the region as well as the countries. To this end, real time sharing of intelligence, better surveillance of the seas to ensure that vessels do not go unnoticed and unmonitored are few of the steps the country can take in safeguarding its waters. Further taking maritime environmental protection into consideration, Sri Lanka needs to ensure that merchant shipping vessels adhere to international laws including those on environmental protection. Sri Lanka can take an active role in safeguarding and ensuring this, thus alleviating a threat posed to its environment.

As much as it is beneficial for countries to cooperate with one another in eliminating and countering terrorist activities, the strengths which each state possesses also has to be kept in mind. Whilst embarking on partnerships, the states have to respect the sovereignty and territorial integrity of the other state, even if it was attempting to safeguard the same area of interest. To this end, Sri Lanka can take advantage of its expertise in the areas of maritime security and counter-terrorism.

Therefore it is the responsibility of states that are in the IOR or are its users to cooperate through the Indian Ocean Rim Association (IORA), and other established mechanisms[28] to safeguard the maritime safety and security of all states, despite its size. The IORA can also utilise the expertise and mechanisms available under the Indian Ocean Marine Affairs Cooperation (IOMAC) and other such agencies with a mandate to operate in this region. Sri Lanka situated centrally in this significant region can take the lead in ensuring safe navigation of commercial vessels among other initiatives. Further all states with naval capabilities and interests can have enhanced naval cooperation with one another to mitigate threats to the security of not merely the states, but also of goods and services transiting the world's lifeline.

Notes

1 HARIHARAN, R. (2013). Sri Lanka And Maritime Security. *Colombo Telegraph.* 9th September. Available from: https://www.colombotelegraph.com/index.php/sri-lanka-and-maritime-security/ [Accessed: 26 September 2015]

2 Ibid.

3 WIJEGUNARATHNE, R. C. (2012). "Maritime Security Concerns in the Indian Ocean: Sri Lanka's Perception of Overcoming Challenges". *Galle Dialogue.* Available from: http://galledialogue.lk/assets/Research_Papers/2012/rear_admiral_rc_wijegunarathne.pdf [Accessed: 26 September 2015]

4 Hambantota Port – officially known as the Magampura Mahinda Rajapaksa Port – is the newest addition to Sri Lanka's maritime capability. The port is being developed as a multi-purpose, industrial and service port under the socio-economic development process of Sri Lanka. Its location on the Southern tip of Sri Lanka within 19 km of east-west shipping route adds strategic value to the port. The port was opened in November 2010 when the first phase of development was completed at a cost of $361 million. Once the entire project is completed, it will provide bunkering, ship repair, ship building and crew change facilities on completion.

5 KAPLAN, R. D. (2010). *Monsoon: The Indian Ocean and the Future of American Power.* New York: Random House.

6 HASHIMI, Zia-ur-Rehman. (Undated) "US Policy in South Asia". The Institute of Strategic Studies Islamabad. Available from: <http://www.issi.org.pk/old-site/ss_Detail.php?dataId=166> [28 August 2012]

7 High Commissioner for Sri Lanka to India Prasad Kariyawasam, at the Public Forum organised by the Kerala International Centre on June 13, 2012. Available from: <http://www.dailynews.lk/2012/06/29/fea01.asp> (29 June 2012)

8 KAPLAN, Monsoon.

9 Ibid

10 KURUKULASURIYA, L. (2011). The Indian Ocean, maritime security and regional undercurrents. *Sunday Times.* [Online] 20th November. Available from: http://www.sundaytimes.lk/111120/Columns/Lasandak.html [Accessed: 26 September 2015]

11 Trincomalee harbour is the second best natural harbour in the world. An ambitious project to develop Trincomalee port and industrial complex is

underway. In June 2012, Sri Lanka signed a $4 billion foreign direct investment (FDI) deal with an Indian company – Gateway Industries - for the Trincomalee Development Project involving development of a deep water jetty, a bulk commodities terminal, a power plant, and a host of other heavy industries and complementary industries in the Sampur area. The project is expected to create more than 5,000 jobs and over 20,000 opportunities for indirect employment.

12 KAPLAN, *Monsoon*.

13 MODI, N. (2015) Text of PM's Address to the Sri Lankan Parliament. 13 March. http://pib.nic.in/newsite/erelease.aspx?relid=86868 [Accessed on 26 September 2015]

14 DE SILVA, Sanath. (2008). "Sharing Maritime Boundary with India: Sri Lankan Experience", paper presented to Near East South Asia Network for Strategic Studies Center. Available from: http://www.kdu.ac.lk/department-of-strategic-studies/images/publications/Sharing_Maritime_BoundarywithIndia-NESA.pdf

15 Sri Lanka Coast Guard. http://www.coastguard.gov.lk/ [Accessed on 28 September 2015]

16 Colombo is annually handling 30.9 million tons of cargo. This makes it one of the top 35 busiest ports of the world. The port's capacities are dramatically increasing with the $1.2 billion expansion project undertaken in 2008 finishing. It would add four new terminals with three berths each. And its container handling capacity is poised to go up from 4.1 million TEUs (Twenty-foot Equivalent Units) to about 12 million TEUs. Colombo is also likely to become one of the few ports in South Asia to receive mega container carriers of 18,000 TEU.

17 Sri Lanka Customs. http://www.customs.gov.lk/overview.html [Accessed on 28 September 2015)

18 WIJEGUNARATHNE, "Maritime Security Concerns"

19 KAPLAN, *Monsoon*.

20 INDI.CA. (2015) Sri Lanka's Rising Sea Level (With Maps) Available from: http://indi.ca/2015/09/sri-lankas-rising-sea-level-with-maps/ [Accessed: 26 September 2015]

21 SIRIWEERA, W. I. and Sanath de Silva. (2013) "Cooperative Security Framework of South Asia: A Sri Lankan Perspective". *Cooperative Security Framework for South Asia*. Ed. Nihar Nayak. New Delhi: IDSA. p.94-98

22 WEERAMANTRY, C.G. (2009) *A Call for National Reawakening*. Pannipitiya: Stamford Lake.

23 KAPLAN, *Monsoon*.

24 Ibid

25 SIRIWEERA and De Silva. "Cooperative Security Framework"

26 'Study on National Strategy for Maritime Security unveiled', Ministry of Foreign Affairs, 02 July 2008 http://www.mea.gov.lk/index.php/media/news-archive/1315-study-on-national-strategy-for-maritime-security-unveiled [Accessed on 22 September 2015)

27 KAPLAN, *Monsoon*.

28 Other established organisations/institutions amongst others include the ASEAN Regional Forum (ARF), South Asian Association for Regional Cooperation (SAARC), Council for Security Cooperation in the Asia Pacific (CSCAP), Asia Pacific Economic Community (APEC), South Asia Regional Port Security Cooperative (SARPSCO), Indian Ocean Naval Symposium (IONS) and the Galle Dialogue.

Indian Ocean Region: Need to Step-up Cooperation

G. V. C. Naidu

Abstract

As the Indian Ocean begins to gain considerable strategic and economic salience, the global maritime centre of gravity is gradually but invariably moving to the Indian Ocean. However, a major shortcoming of the region is poor intra-regional cooperation. Besides a fundamental review of approach to substantially augment cooperation, it is time IORA acquired a more proactive role by undertaking numerous initiatives. Besides undertaking tangible measures with respect to blue economy and efforts to involve extra-regional powers more purposefully, a comprehensive plan aimed at disaster risk reduction could be taken up since the island and rim countries are most prone to disasters. Since sub regions constitute the most potent components in the Indian Ocean, promoting greater interactions among them would go a long way in creating a distinct Indian Ocean identity and a sense of belongingness without which it is difficult to realise the full potential of this region.

Introduction

For all the talk about the rise of the Indian Ocean, there is very little to boast about when it comes to actual cooperation within the region. Indeed, promoting cooperation among the Indian Ocean littorals has been the principal objective since the launch of the regional multilateral mechanism in the mid-1990s in the form of the Indian Ocean Rim Association for Regional Cooperation (IOR-ARC)[1], which has since been renamed as Indian Ocean Rim Association (IORA). However, not much attention was paid till recently to ways, means and areas of cooperation in economic, security and other spheres. Consequently, the weakest link in the discourse

23

on the Indian Ocean is rather tardy progress on regional cooperation. It has to remarkably improve if the Indian Ocean region were to retain and enhance its strategic and economic significance. Fortunately, nearly a couple of decades after the IOR-ARC's founding, the awareness to make use of the geostrategic and geo-economic upside that the Indian Ocean presents is much higher. Secondly, economics and security (here it is primarily referred to traditional security problems) are inter-linked and that one impinges on the other is well understood. Finally, there is also a better appreciation of the fact that cooperation has to be expansive and inclusive and hence a holistic approach has to be evolved.

It, however, must be remembered that promoting robust cooperation is easier said than done given enormous diversity and vast distances that separate the sub-regions of the Indian Ocean from one another because there is a strong tendency among policymakers and analysts alike to view the Indian Ocean region not as one composite region but comprising several sub-regions. Probably the only connection that linked the region in the past had been India and its interactions with most countries along with rim. Nonetheless, these links were neither uniform nor consistent, varied widely, and were sporadic, except with some regions such as Southeast Asia, which had always been much stronger and lasted for more than two millennia. Skills and knowledge were transmitted through this region, and civilizations, cultures, languages, religions, ideas and commerce and trade interactions flowed back and forth from one end to the other seamlessly are visible even today. On the other hand, India's links with the Persian Gulf and the eastern and southern Africa had been episodic. In any case, all these were fundamentally disrupted with the onset of colonialism. It must, however, be granted that the British, who controlled much of the Indian Ocean region, were to an extent instrumental in bringing the sub-regions together. However, these links were tenuous and basically created to serve the colonial interests as compared to the previous relationships that mutually beneficial and free-flowing. Consequently, the British had maintained strong connections at the cost of pre-existing inter-regional linkages thus contributing to further segregation of sub-regions from each other. Whatever the colonial links were that existed among the sub-regions, they virtually diminished with the cold war engulfing much of the region. That has changed dramatically firstly with the end of the cold war, secondly due to the phenomenal rise of East Asia, especially China and to a lesser extent India, and finally the Indian Ocean rim gradually becoming economically a vibrant region. Indeed, the revival of Indo-Pacific as a framework of analysis owes to the rise of the Indian Ocean from being the global backwaters to becoming geo-strategically and economically a pivotal region and its close nexus with West Pacific. As a result, the Indian Ocean does not merely represent vital sea lines of communications alone but as a region that is economically thriving.

Unlike in the past, economics and security are innately inter-linked and they go hand in hand partly because of compulsions of globalisation and partly due to growing intra-regional economic interdependence. It needs no reiteration that, after East Asia, the Indian Ocean Region is economically the most vibrant region endowed with vast natural resources and a huge and rapidly expanding market. After shunning any discussion for a long time, now security issues are no more off IORA's agenda, which hopefully would lead to an extensive debate and crafting of concrete plans. Hence, it is about time creative ideas are thought of to boost cooperation across many spheres. Instead of IORA as an overarching organization, it may be necessary to create a variety of specialized and effective mechanisms under the aegis of the Association to achieve greater cooperation. Against this backdrop, in the following an attempt is made to highlight four specific areas that could help in realizing the above objectives.

IORA's Role in Promoting Economic Cooperation

For a long time, it had been customary to view regions as politically or socially constructed. However, it needs to be recognized that increasingly regions are economically constructed but their success depends on how strongly they are backed politically. Besides intense globalization, across the world economic interests are taking the centre stage and tend to outweigh others and also far more enduring. However, that is where IORA has failed to make a dent despite many opportunities and huge potential. Hence, given that hardly any movement towards trade and investment liberalization within the region has taken place so far, a fundamental shift in thinking and approach is necessary to promote economic cooperation. Since the premise of "Open Regionalism" has failed to promote economic cooperation (as in the case of the Asia Pacific Economic Cooperation) and because creating regional trade blocs by way of Regional Trading Agreements (RTAs) is the new name of the game, a regional identity cannot be sustained unless strongly underpinned by economic cooperation.

Moreover, as the World Trade Organization (WTO) teeters failing to make progress, RTAs are multiplying. The RTAs, both bilateral and regional, are increasingly seen as principal drivers of trade and investment liberalization and economic cooperation. The fact that nearly two-thirds of RTAs have come into existence in the past decade alone is a testimony to their key role and growing significance in world trade. Further, it has been established that RTAs are helping to promote even regional integration with the rapid increase in regional value chains, which, in turn, are playing a crucial role in mitigating numerous security concerns besides promoting common stakes in regional peace and stability. The vast Indo-Pacific region has not seen major wars for more than three and a half decades paralleling ever increasing economic interdependence is a testimony to this. Thus, that there is a close correlation between economic cooperation and security is beyond doubt.

Consequently, much of the focus is shifting to the role of regional and sub regional mechanisms and arrangements as demonstrated by the recent Trans-Pacific Partnership (TPP), ASEAN Economic Community deals and the negotiations on pan-East Asian Regional Comprehensive Economic Partnership (RCEP), which is likely to be launched in 2016. Therefore, it is time IORA got more proactive by taking certain bold steps by fundamentally reorienting the strategy on economic cooperation. It could start working in earnest for a Preferential Trade Agreement (PTA) to begin with, which can lead to trade liberalization among member states. Then move on to other stages step-by-step such as free trade agreement (FTA), customs union, and probably even an economic community. It is ambitious but some beginning needs to be made, for strong economic stakes will be the drivers for greater cooperation in a number of other areas, including security. If a region-wide free trade agreement is difficult, sub-regional arrangements—ASEAN, GCC, SAARC, SADC—could become building blocks, which can be brought together with suitable adjustments for a pan-IOR comprehensive economic cooperation agreement. Based on a Sri Lankan proposal some time back, a concept paper on the feasibility of establishing a PTA and Draft Framework Agreement on the PTA were prepared and a core group comprising Iran, Kenya, Mauritius, Oman, Sri Lanka, Tanzania and Yemen was formed to deliberate on the study, however so far not much progress has taken place.

Blue Economy

It is encouraging that a lot more attention is paid to harness the oceanic living and non-living resources. Instead of exploiting these vast resources indiscriminately, now the challenge is how best it can be done in a sustainable way. Some 300 million people are directly dependent on oceans for their livelihood, and for more than a billion people, mostly in poorer countries, oceans are the principal source for their proteins. Not only oceans are a major source for non-renewable hydrocarbons (over 30 percent are sourced from offshore) but even to harness renewable energy, such as tidal and wind power, oceans are becoming significant.[2] Apart from food and energy security, oceans are becoming critical for seabed minerals, maritime transport, biodiversity conservation, and the management of marine resources. A large number of developing coastal and island nations depend on tourism and fisheries for generation of considerable income. It is established beyond doubt that economic growth and environmental sustainability have to go hand-in-hand. Consequently, "blue economy" is at the heart of development challenges.[3] Developing the ocean economy in a sustainable manner cannot be done by one country but needs to be done at a much a bigger level with close cooperation, especially in the Indian Ocean region.

It is, therefore, laudable that the IORA Council of Ministers' Meeting that was held on 6-9 October 2014 in Perth, Australia adopted the Blue Economy as the top priority. The ministers have identified the following four areas to promote the idea:

(a) **Fisheries and Aquaculture** to ensure food security and contribute to poverty alleviation and sustainable livelihoods;

(b) **Renewable Ocean Energy** to reduce the cost of energy and to mitigate and adapt to the impact of climate change;

(c) **Seaport and Shipping** to promote trade, investment and maritime connectivity in the Indian Ocean Rim region; and,

(d) **Offshore Hydrocarbons and Seabed Minerals** to foster new business opportunities and attract investment in the Indian Ocean.

The Council further reiterated "the importance of IORA's cooperation and engagement with Dialogue Partners, relevant international and regional organizations, the private sector, and civil society in delivering Blue Economy objectives."[4]

Disaster Risk Management

It is well known that the Indian Ocean region is most prone to natural disasters. More than 300,000 people died in the December 2004 Indian Ocean earthquake (and the tsunami that followed). Several thousands died and/or were injured, properties destroyed and livelihood lost or badly disrupted due to Cyclone Nargis which impacted Myanmar in May 2008. The Indian Oceanic islands and littoral countries are thickly populated, and these maritime regions are also very vulnerable to different types of natural disasters. Since most countries along the Indian Ocean rim are relatively poor and developing countries, the human toll and damage to infrastructure tend to be much larger. Moreover, increasingly natural disasters are linked to climate change. Global warming and rising sea levels are already having a devastating effect on island states and coastal regions. Nonetheless, there are no region-wide arrangements for early warning, risk reduction, disaster mitigation, regional responses, and timely relief. Most countries are too small and have limited capacities and hence there is an urgent need to create a variety of information sharing and response mechanisms including joint development of mitigation and post-disaster rehabilitation. Setting up of National Disaster Management Offices and linking them is needed urgently. The IORA is the most appropriate organization to undertake this exercise by involving extra-regional powers such as Japan, which have developed advanced technologies and procedures to deal with natural disasters.

Role of Extra-Regional Great Powers in the Indian Ocean Cooperation

One way or the other, extra-regional powers have always been key players in the Indian Ocean since ancient times. Besides Indians, the Chinese became prominent who expanded trade links with Indians, the Arabs and even with East Africans. The Arabs later on joined by extending their commercial links to India and Southeast Asia and thus constituting a vital link between the Asians and the Europeans. The Europeans soon followed looking for trade opportunities, which resulted in the colonization of the Indian Ocean rim region. In fact, India and China closely interacted since ancient times although much of it was limited to Southeast Asia. However, the awareness about the vast Indian Ocean region was quite evident in the Chinese thinking. A good example was the seven fantastic and massive exploratory voyages by the famed Chinese Admiral Zhang which he undertook in the 15th century during the Ming dynasty to the Indian Ocean, including India, the Middle East and East Africa. The world's most powerful colonial power, Great Britain, probably would not have been that great but for its control virtually over the entire Indian Ocean. In the cold war period, extra-regional powers completely dominated the developments in the Indian Ocean with the U.S. making a strong military presence by taking the place of Britain in the early 1970s at Diego Garcia. Feeble attempts to convert the Indian Ocean as a zone of peace devoid of extra-regional presence was never a feasible idea (nor it is now). So, extra-regional powers have always been part and parcel of the Indian Ocean history.

Opinion on the presence and role of extra-regional great powers is divided and it certainly is a touchy subject in India although perceptions about American military presence have undergone a volte face when compared to the cold war period; it is now seen as contributing to regional security.[5] China is a new entrant seeking ways to protect its interests. Although the 'string of pearls' thesis of building a series of military facilities around India is debunked as an exaggeration[6], New Delhi is concerned about Beijing's long-term intent even as its dependence grows exponentially for its trade and commerce in the Indian Ocean.[7] Given that China's PLA-Navy is yet to become a blue water navy and the limited power projection capabilities that it currently possesses, it may be a long time before it can influence developments in the Indian Ocean. The maritime disputes that China is involved in East and South China Seas are too complex and unlikely to be resolved soon and hence it is likely to get bogged down there. Yet, given its rapidly rising economic and strategic stakes, Beijing cannot be expected to keep away from the Indian Ocean for too long. Japan has actively participated in support of America's counter-terrorism effort in Afghanistan as well as in counter-piracy operations in the Gulf of Aden. Tokyo also has some sort of military facility in strategically located Djibouti lying on the Bab-el-Mandeb Strait, a gateway to the Suez Canal (China too has secured a foothold). Nonetheless, Japan is most unlikely to have a permanent military presence in the Indian Ocean in any significant way. That leaves India and the US and potentially China as major players in the Indian Ocean.

Given their economic heft and growing stakes, the involvement of extra-regional powers in regional development is necessary if the Indian Ocean Rim countries were to make progress on regional cooperation. In many ways, the Indian Ocean owes its rise not simply because it is becoming economically vibrant and is endowed with rich natural resources but also due to the growing role of extra-regional powers and their growing stakes. The boom for commodities in the past two decades would not have been that spectacular had Chinese economy not expanded the way it did logging an average of 10 percent growth rates for nearly three decades. More recently India has joined the ranks of high growth economies after the reforms were introduced in the 1990s. Besides these two large economies, one cannot ignore the fact that the entire East Asian region has witnessed unprecedented growth since the 1980s. Notwithstanding China's slowing economy, the boom in the rest of the region by most indications is likely to continue, and that in many ways would contribute to the Indian Ocean's geostrategic and geo-economic significance.

Perhaps scholars and policymakers also need to pay attention to China's Maritime Silk Road (MSR) initiative. The details of how Beijing seeks to develop infrastructure along major maritime routes are still sketchy, but it is notable that much of it falls within the Indian Ocean. In any case, it is apparent that the Indian Ocean will remain the principal conduit for global economic interactions even as the region itself and the regions around it, especially East Asia, continue to expand their economies. As a result, infrastructure development and other measures to ensure safety and security of movement of goods are vital issues.

Similarly, India has also announced a new initiative called '*Mausam*' to understand how monsoon winds played a critical role in bringing the Indian Ocean countries closer historically leading to cultural exchanges and sharing of knowledge. New Delhi appears to replicate that experience once again. Importantly, China has expressed interest to dovetail its Maritime Silk Road plan to India's *Mausam*. Now, how best these two initiatives can be leveraged to augment regional cooperation in the Indian Ocean region is an issue that deserves greater focus. These apart, there is an urgent need to find ways to evolve cooperative structures at the sub-regional level as well so that their activities could be aligned to that of IORA.

Conclusion

Developments in the Indian Ocean cannot be seen in isolation since it constitutes a crucial link connecting virtually all significant regions of the world one way or another. Whereas the rim is emerging the second fastest growing region in the world, it is also getting integrated into East Asia, which is witnessing profound shifts in its economic and security architecture even as it hogs the global limelight. Indeed, the Indian Ocean's future to a large extent is invariably associated with developments in the West Pacific region. Hence, to better understand the Indian Ocean in perspective, employment of the Indo-Pacific might be more appropriate, for it captures the emerging dynamics between the Indian and Pacific Oceans accurately aside from highlighting the Indian Ocean's overall growing salience.

As the Indian Ocean gains geostrategic and geo-economic significance, the progress in cooperation, especially economic, within the region is abysmal despite huge potential. Unless the littoral states develop strong economic stakes, it is hard to envisage greater cooperation in several other spheres. It is time a fundamental review of approaches to promote cooperation was undertaken. Among several others, two specific areas seem to be promising. One is promoting blue economy on which there is no disagreement that huge oceanic resources need to be exploited for common good but in a sustainable way. Two, disaster risk management since the Indian Ocean is a high-risk region for disasters, both natural and manmade. Substantial intra-regional economic cooperation will lay the foundation for the creation of a unique identity and from a longer run one can envisage the emergence of even an Indian Ocean community.

In this endeavour of stimulating greater cooperation, a partnership with and involvement of extra-regional powers, in particular China, Japan and the US, is essential. These countries have vital interests at stake in the Indian Ocean and without their active participation it is difficult to expect much progress on regional cooperation. They already are Dialogue Partners of IORA and hence the existing institutional mechanisms need to be geared to take full advantage of the strengths of these powers.

It needs to be acknowledged that the Indian Ocean has yet to emerge as a unified and closely interconnected region because it is still compendium of several sub-regions, nations and islands, and the interlinkages in most cases are tenuous. Hence, it is necessary to engage sub-regions more actively. Furthermore, the numerous sub-regional multilateral mechanisms could be brought together on issues of common interest under the aegis of IORA. To make IORA an effective regional multilateral organization, major countries such as India, Australia, Indonesia, South Africa, Malaysia, Iran, Thailand, and Singapore, among others, have to take tangible steps to promote greater cooperation by making issues related to economic development and cooperation a top priority, for economic stakes tend to be biggest incentives. Finally, there is also a need to create an overarching academic center not only to act as an incubation centre for academics, intellectuals and others but also to feed ideas to policymakers, which is sorely missing.

Notes

1   For a detailed assessment of IOR-ARC, see G.V.C. Naidu, "Prospects for IOR-ARC regionalism: an Indian perspective", *Journal of Indian the Ocean Studies* (London), Vol. 8, No. 1 (June 2012).

2   Naoyuki Toyoma, Indian Ocean nations eye stronger 'blue economy", Nikkei Asian Review, April 17, 2014, http://asia.nikkei.com/magazine/20140417-Economic-reboot/Politics-Economy/Indian-Ocean-nations-eye-stronger-blue-economy

3   S.K. Mohanty, et al, Prospects of Blue Economy in the Indian Ocean (New Delhi: RIS, 2015), http://www.ris.org.in/sites/default/files/pdf/Final_Blue_Economy_Report_2015-Website.pdf

4   *Declaration of the Indian Ocean Rim Association on enhancing Blue Economy Cooperation for Sustainable Development in the Indian Ocean Region,* September 3, 2015, http://www.tralac.org/news/article/8036-declaration-of-the-indian-ocean-rim-association-on-enhancing-blue-economy-cooperation-for-sustainable-development-in-the-indian-ocean-region.html

5   G. V. C. Naidu, "India and the Indian Ocean" in Ajaya Das, ed., *India-ASEAN Defence Relations*, (Singapore: RSIS, 2015).

6   See for instance, Ashley S. Townshend, "Unraveling Chinas String of Pearls ", *YaleGlobal*, 16 September 2011, http://yaleglobal.yale.edu/content/unraveling-

chinas-string-pearls?utm_source=ListServe&utm_campaign=cb9e54bce0-YG_ListServe9_15_2010&utm_medium=email

7   Shiv Shankar Menon, "Maritime Imperatives of Indian Foreign Policy" speech at the National Maritime Foundation", 11 September 2009, http://www.maritimeindia.org/sites/all/files/pdf/SMenon.pdf

Biblography

Ashin Das Gupta, *India and the Indian Ocean World: Trade and Politics* (Oxford: Oxford University Press, 1987)

Ashin Das Gupta, Michael Naylor Pearson, *India and the Indian Ocean, 1500-1800* (Oxford: Oxford University Press, 2004)

Dennis Rumley, Sanjay Chaturvedi, Mat Taib Yasin, eds., *The Security of Sea Lanes of Communication in the Indian Ocean Region* (London: Routledge, 2007)

Jivanta Schottli, *Power, Politics and Maritime Governance in the Indian Ocean* (London: Routledge, 2015)

John F. Prevost, *Indian Ocean* (Edina, ABDO Publishing Company, 2010)

Lipi Ghosh, *Eastern Indian Ocean: Historical Links to Contemporary Convergences* (New Castles upon Tyne, Cambridge Scholars Publishing, 2011)

Manoj Gupta, *Indian Ocean Region: Maritime Regimes for Regional Cooperation* (Heidelberg: Springer Science & Business Media, 2010)

Michael N. Pearson, *The Indian Ocean history* (London: Routledge, 2003)

Milo Kearney, *The Indian Ocean in World History* (London: Routledge, 2004)

Robert Kaplan, *Monsoon: The Indian Ocean and the Battle for Supremacy in the 21st Century* (New York: Random House, 2010)

Rong Wang and Suiping Zhu, *Annual Report on the Development of International Relations in the Indian Ocean Region* (Heidelberg: Springer, 2015)

Saji Abraham, *China's Role in the Indian Ocean: Its Implications on India's National Security* (New Delhi: Vij Books India Pvt Ltd, 2015)

Indian Ocean Region: Toward a Zone of Peace and Cooperation Initiative

Francis A. Kornegay, Jr.

Abstract

There is a compelling case to be made for a Zone of Peace and Cooperation in the Indian and Pacific Oceans (PACINDO). As such, it is proposed that the Zone of Peace and Cooperation in the South Atlantic (ZPCSA) be examined as a model for adapting in forging interregional cooperation architecture building on earlier notions of a zone of peace from both an Asian and African vantage-points. Here, the India-Africa connection becomes central. Africa is critical in as much as the continent's littoral and small island states are integral to vetting such a possibility for the Indian Ocean proper. Treatment here begins by examining 'zone of peace and cooperation' prospects in terms of the Indo-Pacific, taking in the Pacific as well as Indian Ocean. It then expands into elaborating such a concept as one option that might emerge from within the India-Africa Summit Forum (IASF) platform.

Introduction

This analysis is intended as a geopolitical exploring of possibilities for forging an inter- regional cooperation architecture for safety and security building on earlier notions elaborating a zone of peace and cooperation from Asian and African vantage-points. The Zone of Peace and Cooperation in the South Atlantic (ZPCSA) is suggested as a possible model for adapting to the Afro-Asian Indo-Pacific. Thus, the African connection is critical in as much as the continent's littoral and small island states are integral to vetting such a possibility for the Indian Ocean proper. Here, the India-Africa nexus becomes the point-of-departure.

This dimension forms the latter part of this analysis which was

34

intended for addressing issues in preparation for the fourth India-Africa Summit Forum (ISAF) convened in New Delhi, 26-29 October 2015. First, however, there is need to examine zone of peace and cooperation prospects in terms of the Indo-Pacific based on the consultation convened by the National Maritime Foundation just prior to ISAF-IV.

To begin with, the changing security environment in the Indian Ocean might be depicted as reflecting the interrelated geopolitical dynamics of different regional subsystems comprising *the continental-maritime interface* defining the Indian Ocean Rim (IOR). These encompass an interregional strategic landscape spanning the rim perimeter from the African and Middle East-West Asian littorals and hinterlands of the western ocean into its eastern rim extending into the Indo-Pacific. As such, it is important to discern the interplay of dynamics shaping this environment against the backdrop of existing organizational actors in the absence of an overarching architecture of cooperation in the IOR. Essentially, this interplay reflects attention focused on perceived rivalries, resulting power-balancing in and along the rim. This extends from the Red Sea/Gulf of Aden and Persian Gulf in the west into Indo-Pacific preoccupations with Sino-territoriality regarding the East and South China Seas.

This context seems to reflect a security environment governing the interplay of great power interactions in this maritime space.[1] Within this calculus, given India's overriding threat perceptions regarding China, accompanied by ambivalence over Beijing's geo-economic diplomacy via its Maritime Silk Route (MSR) vision (back up by the prospective Asian Infrastructure Investment Bank),this analysis attempts to build on a prior proposal offered earlier this year at the Institute for Defence and Security Analyses (IDSA) Asian Security Conference.[2] Suggestion was made that an India-Indonesia strategic partnership be elaborated as a proactive initiative intended to mediate the IOR safety and security environment.[3]

The India-Indonesian SAARC-ASEAN Equation

Here, the two respective regional maritime powers might jointly explore prospects of nurturing greater interregional cooperation between the South Asian Association for Regional Cooperation (SAARC) and the Association of Southeast Asian Nations (ASEAN). (However, a caveat is in order: India's blocking Pakistan from becoming a member of IORA. This stance seems problematic in terms of interregional community-building on 'safety and security' in the Indian Ocean.) It might also be considered that closer collaboration between the SAARC and ASEAN with the African Union (AU) and its regional economic communities of eastern and southern Africa and Indian Ocean Small Island States (IOSIS) might further such a prospect; this would involve the building of a multilateral interface in the western ocean addressing safety and security challenges, anti-piracy being prominent among them.

It would also include interacting with and mutually capacitating the AU's integrated maritime security strategy (AIMS). This is where closer collaboration between South Africa, within the IBSAMAR platform, Kenya, the small island states like Mauritius as well as India, Indonesia and Australia might possibly add value. From India's vantage-point of centrality in the Indian Ocean, this would require a 'look' and 'act west' balancing of its Indo-Pacific oriented 'Act East' policy.

Within the eastern ocean, closer SAARC-ASEAN cooperation could potentially serve as the center piece in fleshing out a *Zone of Peace and Cooperation in the Indian and Pacific Ocean* initiative building on Indonesia's 'Pacific and Indian Ocean' PACINDO concept.[4] ZPC-Pacindo could constitute the Afro-Asian complement to the already elaborated (but underdeveloped) Zone of Peace and Cooperation in the South Atlantic (ZPCSA) – as well as reinforcing the ASEAN-related Zone of Peace, Freedom and Neutrality (ZOPFAN). Such a maritime commons-based architecture in the southern hemisphere would begin to establish some semblance of a balancing equilibrium between global North and South with a networking framework for coordination between different organizations and initiatives (especially since the idea of a joint IORA-IONS safety and security committee seems not to have gelled into a mutually agreed mechanism amongst the member states of both groupings).

Flies in the Ointment

However, the geopolitics of such a scenario is not without complications. The low profile weakness of the SAARC amid outstanding issues between India and Pakistan and China's economic diplomacy among SAARC members are complicating factors; these are accompanied by challenges to the cohesiveness of the ASEAN. Taken together, these challenges problematize such an elaborated Zone of Peace & Cooperation possibility. However, simply revisiting a latter day 'Zone of Peace' in the Indian Ocean

(IOPZ) as a declaration first raised by Sri Lanka in 1970 without elaborating it into an architecture of cooperation for already existing IORA and IONS initiatives may not be sufficient in managing the interregional safety and security environment as a priority Indian security interest.[5]

Revisiting this initiative may be instructive especially in terms of a continental-maritime conceptual framework: "...A comprehensive definition of peace zone, according to Sri Lanka's memorandum submitted to the Singapore Conference Commonwealth Prime Ministers in January 1971, should cover not merely the Indian Ocean proper but the land areas, air space and territorial waters of the littoral and hinterland states of the Indian Ocean. By extending the scope of peace zone to the land mass, all forms of militarization, areas under build-up and nuclear weapons programme could be brought under its purview."[6] A companion initiative was the 'Zone of Peace Nuclear Free Zone' (ZOPFAN), similar to that which inspired the South Atlantic initiative.[7]

The thinking of the time, foreshadowing today was captured in the following terms: "The arguments used in the 1970s and 1980s by littoral and island states to maintain or increase their military strength related to the protection and exploitation of the resources of the ocean. If these countries were not successful in ensuring their own security, in defining their own interest and in cooperating economically, militarily and politically, the initiatives proposed for IOPZ and ZOPFAN could leave the way open for the domination of the Indian Ocean by the People's Republic of China. Such domination might not only be political, but might also extend to the exploitation of the ocean's biotic and mineral resources."[8]

This is where I think the question of the effectiveness of revisiting these earlier initiatives may need focusing given the increasing focus on Blue Economy agendas, but also a need to transcend 'zero-sum' great power rivalry logic. This is why India's strategic imagination might need to consider balancing 'Act East' toward Southeast Asia where Indonesia is the 'global maritime axis' with a 'Whole of Indian Ocean' policy that more actively engages western Indian Ocean actors in the Persian Gulf and along with African littoral. The desired end result of such engagements should be a harmonizing of regional and sub-regional interests and initiatives for all regional and extra-regional stakeholders in the Indian Ocean space irrespective of parochial great power pressures being exerted in their own interest.

This relates especially to India, Indonesia and South Africa where the bottom-line is one in which whomever proactively assumes the initiative in defining terms of interregional engagement (as opposed to reacting to others initiatives) will be those who gain and retain the initiative in shaping the security environment and its geostrategic landscape as well as the terms of cooperation. Here, the Zone of Peace and Cooperation in the South Atlantic (ZPCSA) might serve as a model for adapting to the whole of Indo-Pacific environment.

Taking a Page from the South Atlantic

Founded in 1986 by United Nation General Assembly Resolution A/RES/41/11 at Brazil's initiative, its focus: Preventing the geographical proliferation of nuclear weapons and of reducing and eventually eliminating the military presence of countries from other regions. As a 'nuclear-weapon-free zone' it has expanded to promote dialogue and South-South Cooperation. It is considered precursor to the establishing of IBSA, seen as one of the outcomes of ZPCSA. It's Plan of Action adopted in Luanda, Angola in 2007 proposes to: "...generate cooperation mechanisms with visible results addressing environmental issues, air and sea terminals security, mapping and exploration of the sea bed and combating transnational organized crime."[9] These aims anticipated IORA's current Blue Economy focus.

For similar reasons, what started out as the IORA-IONS joint safety and security committee might be considered one key component of a forerunner to motivating a more elaborated interregional ZPCSA-like architecture of coordination in Indian and Pacific Ocean safety and security matters. To be sure, this will require a careful sorting out of what is discrete and that which is overlapping in the search for synergy between 'safety' and 'security' domains.

The main point, however, is that the ZPCSA is a multilateral membership organization, not a resolution or declaration that, in its repetitiveness without follow-up action, loses its relevance. ZPCSA encompasses 24 member states with a Plan of Action adopted in Luanda, Angola in 2007, including the following areas of cooperation include:

- Economic and commercial cooperation;

- Promote trade and investment;

- Scientific and technical cooperation;

- Initiatives of a political and diplomatic nature;

- Environmental protection;

- Conflict resolution;

- Mechanism for member states to coordinate on a number of fronts.[10]

Anticipating by several years the current Blue Economy agenda, these programmatic areas of multilateral engagement are illustrative of the scope of engagement that could be fleshed for the Indian and Pacific Oceans in networking functional cooperation within IORA while sorting out the parameters of safety and security with IONS and other initiatives. Of course, from comparative perspectives, the security environments among regions and sub-regions in the South Atlantic and the Indian Ocean are quite different in as much as post-cold war regional and external great power rivalries are virtually absent in the South Atlantic compared to the Indian Ocean.

That is, save for the very real Falklands-Malvinas stalemate between the UK and Argentina and the dilemmas this creates for ZPCSA members. Post-cold war, the apartheid-inspired promotion of a NATO-aligned 'South Atlantic treaty organisation' never materialised, though ironically, a similar idea was raised by the late Venezuelan leader Hugo Cesar Chavez and Muammar al-Qaddafi at an African-South American summit in Caracas in 2009.

Though Brazil was the major impetus behind ZPCSA, it's only in more recent years that this initiative is been seen as having begun to receive a higher level of priority in Brasilia's calculus. As in the case of India, this has tracked Brazil's growing preoccupation with exerting a regional leadership as an emerging power. Brazil's regional representational role in the BRICS forum as well as its trilateral relationship with India and South Africa in IBSA is indicative as it seeks permanent membership at the UN Security Council 'high table.' In a related vein, Brazil has been a prime mover in the emergence of the Union of South American States (UNASUR) and a 'South American Defence Council.'

There is, however, concern as to whether or not Brazil has the economic and financial capacity to project a more robust maritime security role in the South Atlantic, given the ebb the economy, along with other BRICS members, have been experiencing. This flagging momentum on the economic front is matched by observations of long delays in consummating bilateral agreements in the maritime area due to the lengthy process such agreements are subjected to in the Brazilian Congress. Thus, a maritime South multilateralism giving greater operational impetus to the ZPCSA remains a challenge.

Apart from the Gulf of Guinea on the African side of the ocean, the geopolitical security environment in the South Atlantic is comparatively more benign than in the Indian and Pacific Ocean cockpits of great power rivalries. Moreover, feeding into the Indian and Pacific Ocean interregional domains are important regional subsystems dynamics. These include: the Red Sea and Persian Gulf back-dropping Northeast African and Middle Eastern along the Somali Coast, including the regionalized civil war in Yemen turmoil in the western Indian Ocean; while west of the small Indian Ocean island states that form part of off-shore eastern and southern Africa are the southern Asian dynamics of the Straits of Malacca leading into the Indo-Pacific realms of increasing tensions in the Yellow, East and South China Seas.

However, because of this more complicated security environment, those areas cited in the ZPCSA such as "initiatives of a political and diplomatic nature" and 'conflict resolution" along with its functional areas of cooperation should resonate in informing a similar zone of peace and cooperation architecture adapted to the Indian and Pacific Oceans circumstances. Hence, studying the ZPCSA experience as a point of departure for transforming zone of peace resolutions and declarations into operationalizing a multilateral cooperation agenda should reflect a compelling logic for taking action. Closely related, in this regard, are issues of multilateral interfacing among Asian and African Indian Ocean Rim states which informed some of the discussions leading up to the fourth India-Africa Summit Forum (IASF) convened in New Delhi on October 26th.

Indo-African Multilateral Interfacing

The case for transforming repetitive zone of peace declarations into an operational ZPCSA-type structure was the centrepiece of this author's presentation at the Indian Council on World Affairs (ICWA) conference on IASF IV held back-to-back with the National Maritime Foundation IORA safety and security conference. As such, much of this presentation is recapitulated here. It located the interregional implications of an Indian and Pacific Ocean zone of peace and cooperation architecture within the ambit of an Indo-African multilateral interfacing. This would have to address the regionalization challenges in Africa and South Asia pertaining to the needed strengthening of regional economic communities (RECs).

Here, the modalities of multilateral interfacing based on the challenges facing African RECs on the one hand and the SAARC on the other form an important backdrop but not necessarily an obstacle to fleshing out an Indian and Pacific Oceans zone of peace and cooperation initiative.From a geostrategic standpoint, multilateral interfacing between Africa and India may need to factor in four critical modalities of interaction:

- 1st, elevating the SAARC into a more robust regional economic community (possibly generating momentum for that 'South Asian Free Trade Area'?) that can fill the niche of connectivity between the eastern and southern Africa Tripartite 'Cape to Cairo' Free Trade Area (TFTA) and the recently launched ASEAN Economic Community.

- 2nd, establishing closer links between the AU and the SAARC comparable to that between the SAARC and the European Union (EU) leading eventually to a *Trilateral Economic Communities Partnership*: the eastern and southern African TFTA-SAARC-ASEAN.

- 3rd, a strengthened bilateral relationship between India and South Africa, interacting with a needed coming to terms with the future of the trilateral relationship among themselves and Brazil within IBSA as a complement to their relationship within BRICS and how this can serve India's African and vice versa agenda.

- 4th, an India-African Indian Ocean Rim diplomacy linked to the building of an Indian and Pacific Ocean's zone of peace and cooperation between eastern and southern African economic communities, SAARC and ASEAN, revisiting the idea of an Afro-Asian trilateral economic community's partnership. Here, the Persian Gulf will also need to be factored into such a scenario.

Apart from the close intersection between these 4 overlapping modalities of engagement, the premise of the approach suggested in this presentation is that multilateral inter-regionalism should be prioritized in generating momentum for "structural reforms of existing institutions of global trade and governance." The assumption informing this premise is the presumed efficacy of regionalism and interregional cooperation as bottom-up 'building blocks' in fleshing out an architecture of South-South Cooperation within the context of strengthening global governance. A related premise in this regard is that within a multipolar international landscape, global economic integration is evolving along regional and overlapping realms of interregional interaction into a 'federalist' reconfiguring of the world's geopolitical-economy: *Global Economic Federalism*.[11]

As such, this 'federalization' of the global economy reflects what might be billed as 'The Rise of the RECs' – the emergence of regional economic communities (RECs). Thus, it is held here that prospects for a multilateral consolidating of India-Africa relations may best be served by the joint nurturing of an interface revolving around the strengthening of Asian and African RECs interacting with ever greater interregional cooperation. In this regard, the Indian Ocean Rim forms a natural space within which Afro-Asian relations can evolve along such patterns of multilateralism and, in the process, influence the emergence of the Indian Ocean as the major locus around which SSC flourishes, in effect, a joint India-Africa fashioning of an Indian Ocean Multilateral System (IOMS).

The Indian Ocean Nexus: 'Act West'

Eastern and southern Africa form the natural point-of-departure for multilateral interfacing. Thus, regarding security cooperation, a multilateral zone of peace and cooperation framework, while serving as a means of managing and keeping to a minimum great power rivalries in the western Indian Ocean, would reinforce the strategic presence India has and needs to further develop with African littoral and island states. These include its bilateral defence assistance agreement with Mauritius authorizing India to patrol its Exclusive Economic Zone and India's listening post in northern Madagascar for monitoring shipping in the western ocean. Reported plans for 'trilateral' security cooperation involving the US and India in African peacekeeping capacity-building can reinforce this trend.

Both, in economic and security terms, such engagement between India and Africa presupposes India moving toward a 'Look and Act West' policy in the western Indian Ocean as complementary to its 'Act East' policy toward Southeast Asia. Here, India's potential axis with South Africa within their IBSA and BRICS memberships can be starting points in elaborating such a balance between western and eastern spheres of the Indian Ocean. In this regard, attention might be given to how the IBSAMAR naval exercises could be expanded to include other African navies or to how India might explore developmental naval exercises with other states along the African littoral of the Indian Ocean.

The regionalization of India-Africa relations as a multilateral interfacing scenario where RECs become focal points of engagement both in economic, developmental and security cooperation terms may hold out substantial promise in generating ever greater momentum in relations between Africa and India. The end point of Indo-African multilateral interfacing with respect to the Indian Ocean might focus on *convening a summit of African and Asian regional economic communities bordering the Indian Ocean Rim as well as island states.*

It should be inclusive of interregional structures like IORA and IONS to elaborate a zone of peace and cooperation framework informed by the Brazilian-initiated ZPCSA. Perhaps a 'quadrilateral' of South Africa, India, Indonesia and Australia meeting in Mauritius could, at some point in the future of political and diplomatic will, get the ball rolling. From a purely African perspective such an initiative should be seen in the broader continental context informing an ongoing organized zone of peace and cooperation strategic vision.

Africa, after all is encircled by maritime domains from north to south, east to west. As such, an Indian (and Pacific) Oceans focus that addresses India's concerns might be the point-of-departure for a broader initiative involving a civil society-intergovernmental partnership establishing a *Zone of Peace and Cooperation Forum.* It's purpose would be to promote the development of Zones of Peace in the southern oceans by advocating the elaboration of the Zone of Peace in the Indian and Pacific Oceans from constantly reiterated declarations into a multilateral platform initiative on par with the Zone of Peace and Cooperation in the South Atlantic; 2) promote the strengthening of the ZPCSA as the ongoing multilateral South-South cooperation platform between African-South American (ASA) summits and to share experiences with Indian Ocean Rim (IOR) countries; and consider prospects for getting underway a zone of peace and cooperation dialogue in the Mediterranean.

Notes

1   This was the theme of a volume published in 2015 by Shipra Publications titled *Evolving Dynamics in the Indian Ocean: prospects and the Way Forward* edited by Captain Raghavendra Misha who organised a symposium under this theme in February March 2014 hosted by the National Maritime Foundation of India, New Delhi.

2   The paper delivered at that 17th Asian Security Conference, February 11-13, 2015 on the theme 'Asian Security: Comprehending the Indian Approach' organised by the Institute for Defence and Security Analyses (IDSA) is titled 'Deciphering Oriental Mysteries of Silk, Pearls & Diamonds: Maritime dimensions of India's Strategic dilemmas in the changing Asian power balance.' Publication is in process.

3   In this paper it was suggested that there should be considered the operationalizing of declarations calling for a 'Zone of Peace in the Indian Ocean' into an India-Indonesian led 'Zone of Peace and Cooperation in the Indian and Pacific Oceans' similar to the South Atlantic Zone of Peace and Cooperation (ZPCSA) that Brazil initiated.

4   See: "Jokowi launches maritime doctrine to the world" *Jakarta Post*, November 13, 2014. Also: 'PACINDO – European Sting – Critical News & Insights,' April 18, 2015 and a critique: "Indonesia's Asian Fulcrum Idea: A new proposal exposes the inconsistency in Jakarta's worldview," by Vibhanshu Shekar, *The Diplomat*, July 24, 2015.

5   Abhijit Singh,"The Indian Ocean Zone of Peace: Sifting 'fact' from 'illusion'," IDSA Comment, December 19, 2014.

6   Kamal Kumar, Indian Ocean as a Zone of Peace: problems and Prospects. APH Publishing, 387pp. Page 60.

7   "Nuclear-Weapon-Free Zones" United Nations Office for Disarmament Affairs (UNODA), www.un.org/disarmament/WMD/**Nuclear**/NWFZ.shtml. *Also: "Southeast Asian Nuclear-Weapons-Free Zone (SEANWFZ) Treaty (Bangkok Treaty)," in NTI: Building a Safer World, October 6, 2015.*

8   Vivian Louis Forbes, The Maritime Boundaries of the Indian Ocean, NUS Press, 1995. 267 pp. Page 55.

9   "Twenty four South Atlantic countries meet in Uruguay to promote cooperation," *MercoPress/South Atlantic News Agency*, January 12, 2013.

10 Ibid.

11 Francis A. Kornegay, Jr. "Laying the BRICS of a New Global Order: A conceptual scenario," in *Laying the BRICS of a New Global Order: From Yekaterinburg 2009 to eThekwini 2013,* by Francis A. Kornegay & Narnia Bohler-Muller, eds. Africa Institute of South Africa, 2013, pp. 1-36.

Role of Extra Regional Stakeholders in the Indian Ocean: An Inclusive Approach

Thomas Daniel

Abstract

Maritime safety and security has always been a key concern in the Indian Ocean, especially with the advent of non-traditional threats and increasing risk of its convergence with traditional security concerns. Hence, it is imperative for all stakeholders of the Indian Ocean – both littoral and extra-regional, to adopt a more inclusive approach to maritime safety and security in the Indian Ocean. These include bigger roles for capable external stakeholders in the capacity building of Indian Ocean states and in creating a more inclusive maritime security framework. Existing regional mechanisms like IORA and IONS could be moulded in order to better fit an inclusive approach. In doing so however, stakeholders should consider the extent and viability of ASEAN's involvement in the Indian Ocean and if an ASEAN inspired inclusive approach is best suited for the region. The key outcome for all stakeholders shouldn't just be an inclusive approach to maritime safety and security but one that is effective and comprehensive.

Introduction

This chapter has three main components. First, it will address the need for an inclusive approach to maritime security in the Indian Ocean. Second, it looks at the role of external stakeholders in maritime capacity building and possible norms that the region can adopt from ASEAN in setting up a more inclusive maritime security community. Third, it puts forward two questions which stakeholders in the Indian Ocean region, notably the members and dialogue partners of Indian Ocean Rim Association (IORA), need to ask themselves in their quest for a more inclusive approach to maritime security and safety in the Indian Ocean.

The Indian Ocean region is home to nearly one-third of the world's population and is of high economic and strategic significance due to its location and the traffic that passes through it. Nearly half of the world's container ships, one third of the bulk cargo traffic and two thirds of the world's oil shipments pass through the Indian Ocean[1].

Thus, the sea lanes in the Indian Ocean are central to regional trade and vital to the global economy. As the global economic and strategic balance swings towards Asia with the regional players like China, India and Southeast Asia growing in prominence and importance, the geo-political and geo-economic importance of the Indian Ocean grows with it. The situation takes on added urgency, according to some observers in South Asia, as an economically robust China looks increasingly beyond the South and East China Seas – and even arguably, the Pacific – in order to secure its resource and trade routes.

Maritime security in the Indian Ocean – the Need for Inclusiveness

The immense and diverse Indian Ocean maritime region poses significant security challenges, particularly in devising coordinated, collaborative and inclusive approaches to shared security challenges that transcend national maritime boundaries. Due to the geographical scope and capacity issues, many of these challenges are beyond the sphere and capabilities of any single nation to address.

Similar to the South China Sea, the issues affecting maritime security in the Indian Ocean are multifaceted and complex, running both the gamut of traditional and non-traditional threats. These include issues of sovereignty and the application of international law, freedom of navigation – including that of trade and energy security, the potential of interstate conflict – including those which originate from the Indian Ocean and those that use the region another 'front', conservation and protection of maritime resources and the environment, trans boundary crime, terrorism, and the movements of displaced people amongst others.

While much of the conversation tends to focus on the rise of non-traditional maritime security threats, and rightly so, stakeholders would be wise to keep in mind that traditional and non-traditional security issues increasingly overlap and require multifaceted, inclusive responses. Robert Kaplan famously stated in 2009 that as it becomes more militarised, the Indian Ocean will be a major stage for the security challenges of the twenty-first century. Largely due to concerns over energy security, extra-regional powers are seeking to maintain and extend their presence in the region, thus complicating the overall strategic outlook of the region[2].

Lately, geo-political differences are becoming very evident in the Indian Ocean, particularly between the rising powers of India and China. The established, and some say declining, power of the United States (US) is also thrown into this mix. Changing power dynamics, longstanding territorial disputes in the East and South China Seas, and the US rebalance to Asia have all contributed to issues of maritime safety and security in the Indian Ocean emerging as a key focus area for the region.

While the Indian Ocean may have certain similar maritime security issues as the South China Sea, it lacks a distinctive regional identity linked to a political association or security framework as how ASEAN is interconnected within the South China Sea[3]. According to Cordner's 2014 study on risks and vulnerabilities in the Indian Ocean, there are still no concrete multilateral security architectures and mechanisms specifically designed for dealing with maritime security in the Indian Ocean. This includes security dialogues and cooperation at the government-to-government level. However, there are signs that governments and regional organisations in the region, like the IORA, are moving to address that[4].

Economics, environment and security concerns interact in the Indian Ocean in dynamic and potentially destructive ways. Today the region has generated many well-intentioned but incomplete forms of governance. Existing national, regional and global regimes and mechanisms are not sufficiently robust for the task of maintaining the Indian Ocean as a sustainable zone of commerce, energy security and peace. What is needed, are more inclusive approaches and strategies at the national, regional and global level that can ensure maritime security for all stakeholders.

Capacity Building in the Indian Ocean – Roles for External Stakeholders

Contributions in capacity building are a key role which can see greater involvement of external stakeholders in the Indian Ocean. As stated earlier, the littoral states of the Indian Ocean are remarkably diverse in terms of size, economic, strategic and operational strength and capacity. Not all states have the capacity to fulfil their responsibilities for managing their respective maritime zones, let alone ensuring the security of the wider region[5]. Exploitation, pollution and water-security infringements largely proceed unchecked in many national jurisdictions, and at the high seas. Few regional countries have the capacity to deal with massive human tragedies and environmental damage to coastal areas, which arise from repeated natural disasters.

On the other hand, some of the Indian Ocean extra regional stakeholders are very advanced in terms of capability and capacity when it comes to maritime security. They include major powers, like the US, China, Japan and the European Union, and powerful commercial interests that can aid those less capable stakeholders in capacity building. These can include workshops, training and even aid in the form of the necessary maritime and land assets or financial assistance to better ensure maritime security in the Indian Ocean. Most of these external stakeholders have vested interests in the Indian Ocean and require a secure maritime environment. It is after all more effective to properly train and equip local forces to maintain local maritime safety and security than to deploy foreign forces for extended periods of time.

These extra regional stakeholders can and should support comprehensive capability development and capacity building in regions affected by piracy and other forms of maritime crime, including in ports and coastal waters, in order to enable and enhance the capacity of coastal states and regional maritime security regimes. In some cases, there has to be a re-orientation of foreign assistance to regional states. There should be a convergence of interests between all stakeholders and a commitment to the prosperity of the Indian Ocean which can be attained through ensuring the safety and security of these waters.

A Maritime Security Community in the Indian Ocean – Cues from ASEAN

A significant way to ensure a more inclusive and comprehensive maritime security environment in the Indian Ocean could be by creating a maritime security community for the region. Here, the region can look to ASEAN – a region no less diverse and complicated – for some cues.

An inclusive maritime environment and by extension the safety and security of the maritime domain is a key priority of ASEAN, and its member have worked hard towards that end. The ASEAN Regional Forum (ARF) and the ASEAN Defence Ministers Meeting (ADMM) and the ADMM Plus are key platforms where issues of maritime safety are routinely addressed. Another platform that is more focused on maritime security is the now expanded ASEAN Maritime Forum, which includes the ten member countries plus key partners like Australia, China, India, Japan, New Zealand, South Korea, Russia and the United States.

While ASEAN is by no means the best example of a problem free security architecture – although many in ASEAN will claim that it is a work-in-progress – some of its multilateral security initiatives could offer a guide to Indian Ocean countries – led by India in constructing a viable and inclusive maritime security framework or architecture for the region. The ARF and the ADMM Plus are good examples of top-down models where inclusive, albeit macro discussions are slowly but surely evolving to include policy and technical working groups that have lasting impacts for the region.

IORA and IONS as a Platform for a More Inclusive Security Community

A possible security community could begin with the enhancement of IORA itself and its eventual enmeshment with the Indian Ocean Naval Symposium (IONS).

IORA represents an excellent platform to achieve a more inclusive approach to maritime security and safety in the Indian Ocean and maritime security has now become a key focus area of IORA. To do this however, IORA needs to look at a more holistic approach to the Indian Ocean and to embrace all littoral states and important external stakeholders. Some names that come to mind, which represent key stakeholders who are not yet involved, are Pakistan and Saudi Arabia. Some observers have even suggested that ASEAN as an organisation can also be brought in. There also needs to be significant changes in the way that the IORA functions – an aspect which is discussed in detail later in the chapter.

IONS, represents another promising platform – but not as it stands today. It was initiated by the Indian Navy in 2008 and inspired by the

Western Pacific Naval Symposium. However, much of the focus of IONS has been to build on mutual discussions rather than actions in the form of joint naval operations in the region. Consequently, it can be seen over the years that while IONS has conducted several workshops, seminars and essay competitions, it has yet to conduct a single naval operation under its aegis. India has promoted IONS to foster the necessary cooperation between navies and coast guards in the Indian Ocean region. However, extra-regional countries with significant interests in the region were not invited to participate[6]. While this is understandable given the sensitivity of multilateral operations and regional rivalries, it is a roadblock that the stakeholders should and can overcome.

Several naval analysts have argued that the piracy crisis in the Western Indian Ocean, off the Gulf of Aden was a missed opportunity for IONS to move towards a more inclusive and operationalised platform[7]. While the littoral states of Indian Ocean might not have the naval capacity, some of the dialogue partners of IORA not only have the capacity but experience and interest in strengthening IONS. Greater operationalization of IONS not just on piracy and maritime crime but also on Search And Rescue (SAR), Humanitarian Assistance and Disaster Rescue (HADR), counter terrorism and so on, will have a positive impact on a more inclusive approach to maritime security in the Indian Ocean. Perhaps the time has now come for a 'handshake' between the only two pan-Indian Ocean organisations –IORA and IONS. This could perhaps provide the much needed impetus to the former.

Additionally, this new, inclusive security order could consider incorporating the Indian Navy's biennial Milan exercise. As it stands, the exercise has now expanded to include elements of interoperability in HADR in addition to more traditional combat elements. HADR, along with SAR and elements of counter-piracy are excellent platforms for building avenues of communication, exchanges and eventually, a degree of trust between regional navies. On a positive note, last year's Milan exercise saw the participation of 17 nations – it's highest ever since inception in 1995.

Issues to Ponder

By way of concluding, this chapter will now examine two key questions when it comes to the points raised above and a more inclusive approach to maritime security in the Indian Ocean.

First – the question of ASEAN and the extent of its involvement and interest in the Indian Ocean as an institution. While there have been calls for greater ASEAN involvement in the Indian Ocean, the fact is that ASEAN, and in fact most ASEAN member states – perhaps even those that are members of IORA, view the Indian Ocean and what happens in it as an abstract. Let's face it – how often to policymakers and strategists in ASEAN focus deeply on the Indian Ocean? How often do we hear of conferences and in-depth research in ASEAN on the Indian Ocean that are translated into policy carried out by governments or the regional organisation? The ARF, while having conducted several workshops and discussions on the Indian Ocean has yet to seriously work towards bringing the region into its geographical ambit, or addressing the hard security issues there[8].

There are exceptions to this perhaps in Indonesia, Myanmar and Thailand. In Malaysia, despite some focus on the Indian Ocean and its happenings by certain observers and scholars, domestic strategic conversations on the region only took off in the aftermath of the unfortunate disappearance of flight MH370. As it stands, ASEAN itself is stretched thin and distracted by a multitude of external and internal issues. The ASEAN Community and the South China Sea dispute are but two prominent examples. These exhaustive issues will take up much time, resources and attention by ASEAN and its member states. Failure to manage these issues properly will have longstanding impacts on the very nature of the organisation itself.

Second – is an all-inclusive maritime framework really required in the Indian Ocean? Some stakeholders, including those in the defence establishments might not be so inclined and understandably so. One of the challenges of being too inclusive is that eventually, too much effort might be put into trying to include and appease everyone and the actual problems are never solved. In some cases, they might even be compounded. While inclusive frameworks might work well in dealing with non-traditional threats, it becomes a little sketchier when dealing with longstanding territorial disputes and strategic rivalries.

Again, one need only to look at the South China Sea where despite greater and more inclusive maritime cooperation, China has pressed ahead with massive land reclamations in contested areas and is likely to start building facilities there. Here, I should point out that other ASEAN claimants have also engaged in land reclamation and facility building, though not on the scale of China and before regional norms/principles on the issues had been concretised as per UNCLOS.

As for IORA in particular, it has always prided itself on being a rather loose and informal organisation[9]. If it decides to become more institutionalised in order to bring about a more effective inclusive environment in the Indian Ocean, current practices like consensual decision making could prove to be both a blessing and a curse for the organisation in the long run. Indian Ocean stakeholders must ask themselves if they are prepared to move forward at the pace of its slowest member.

Conclusion

These are but some of the approaches and challenges when it comes to an inclusive approach to maritime security in the Indian Ocean and the roles of and lessons from extra regional stakeholders. While there will be differences of capabilities, ideologies and even disputes, it will be the inclusive nature of regional organisations like the IORA – and its ability to harness it – that will ultimately lead to more inclusive approaches and strategies in the Indian Ocean, not just for maritime safety and security but in all areas of mutual interest. The question then for both littoral states and extra regional stakeholders is not whether an inclusive approach should be adopted or not, but rather, how to go about achieving an inclusive security/safety framework while ensuring that it is as effective as well as comprehensive.

Notes

1   Bergin, A. (2012) Managing the Indian Ocean, The Diplomat, January 5 (Online) Available at: http://thediplomat.com/2012/01/managing-the-indian-ocean/

2   Bateman, S. & Bergin, A. (2011) New challenges for maritime security in the Indian Ocean - an Australian perspective, Journal of the Indian Ocean Region Vol. 7, No. 1, pp. 117-125.

3   Lin, S. & Grundy-Warr, C. (2012) ASEAN and interconnecting regional spheres: Lessons for the Indian Ocean Region, Journal of the Indian Ocean Region, Vol. 8, No.1, pp. 66

4   Cordner, L. (2014) Exploring Risks and Vulnerabilities: An Alternate Approach to Maritime Security Cooperation in the Indian Ocean Region, Journal of Defence Studies, Vol. 8, No. 2, April–June 2014, p.31

5   Cordner, L. (2014): Exploring Risks and Vulnerabilities: An Alternate Approach to Maritime Security Cooperation in the Indian Ocean Region, Journal of Defence Studies, Vol. 8, No. 2, April–June 2014, p.36

6   Cordner, L. (2010) 'Rethinking maritime security in the Indian Ocean Region, Journal of the Indian Ocean Region, Vol. 6, No. 1, June, pp. 67 – 85

7   Upadhyaya S. (2014) Maritime security cooperation in the Indian Ocean Region: The role of the Indian Navy, Australian Journal of Maritime & Ocean Affairs, Vol. 6, No. 4, pp.173-190 (Online) Available at: http://dx.doi.org/10.10 80/18366503.2014.920945

8   Bateman, S. Chan, J. & Graham, E. (2011) ASEAN and the Indian Ocean – A Policy Paper, RSIS, Singapore, p.41

9   DFAT (Australia) (2015) Development of IORA (Online) Available at: http:// dfat.gov.au/international-relations/regional-architecture/indian-ocean/iora/ Pages/development-of-iora.aspx

Addressing Transnational Organised Crime: A Whole of Nation Approach

Martin A. Sebastian

Abstract

The measures being undertaken to address maritime security threats are obviously far from effective. The reasons to this statement are that seaborne smuggling of people, goods and wildlife, illegal fishing and piracy and armed robbery are on the rise. Though it is arguable that these measures are lopsided and that while maritime security agencies blame land security agencies for "sea blindness", maritime security agencies themselves are guilty of "land blindness" where threat assessment and operations are concerned. Lack of coherent measures has impacted intelligence led operations thus raising costs on risk mitigation and crisis response. Inter service rivalry and lack of information sharing has allowed the "big fish to swim in warm waters". Most law enforcement operations have only targeted symptoms instead of the root causes of these crimes.

Introduction

When addressing maritime security, the first thing we need to look at is ourselves and our institutional cultures in order to identify any systemic impediments to achieving effective and persistent national domain awareness. All countries have unique maritime security governance frameworks, for instance some coast guards are part of the navy, while others are separate, while in other smaller coastal nations, the coast guards are the navy. Still, the common trait in all coastal states is that multiple forces, ministries and agencies all have a strong interest in maritime surveillance, whether it's the immigration department for illegal migrants, the national police for counter-narcotics, the fisheries department for illegal fishing, the coast guard for search and rescue, or the navy for sovereign presence and when necessary for combat. When these groups are stove-piped, acting separately, guarding their data jealously, and competing against one another for resources and influence, then they collectively do their countries a disservice, and it becomes much easier for adversaries to identify and exploit the vulnerabilities that exist at the inter-agency seams.

Illegal Cross Border Movements

People Smuggling

Smuggling of migrants is defined by Article 3 of the Migrant Smuggling Protocol supplementing the United Nations Transnational Organized Crime Convention (UNTOC), as "...the procurement, in order to obtain, directly or indirectly, a financial or other material benefit, of the illegal entry of a person into a state party of which the person is not a national." The specific nature of the sea-based component of the smuggling journey resulted in a dedicated section on the issue in the Migrant Smuggling Protocol. While smuggling by sea accounts only for a small portion of overall migrant smuggling around the world, the particular dangers of irregular travel at sea make it a priority for response; though more migrant smuggling occurs by air, more deaths occur by sea.

Attempting to isolate the issue of migrant smuggling by sea from other forms of migrant smuggling is in some ways an artificial and potentially misleading exercise. Migrant smuggling by sea generally occurs as part of a wider smuggling process often involving land and/or air movements. Furthermore, the complex nature of criminal migrant smuggling networks and their modus operandi means that smugglers who use sea routes cannot be identified purely by looking to the sea; the transnational criminal network itself must be traced from a smuggling vessel, back to the coast of embarkation, and from there back to countries of transit and origin.

As with other forms of organized crime, the groups concerned have increased their operations by shifting routes in a bid to expand into other markets and circumvent the responses of States. Criminal groups have merged or formed cooperative relationships, expanding their geographical reach and the range of their criminal activities. Some criminal groups view migrants as simply one of many commodities to be smuggled, alongside drugs and firearms. Since the smuggling of migrants is a highly profitable illicit activity with a relatively low risk of detection, it is attractive to criminals. The absence/inadequacy of national legislation to address the smuggling of migrants in many parts of the world often means that smugglers of migrants can continue to commit the crime with little fear of being brought to justice. Responses by States often target migrants, leaving smugglers, and especially organized criminal groups, which are more difficult to apprehend, to use the sea routes.

Only a limited number of States have specific policies and mechanisms in place aimed at countering the smuggling of migrants, and a lack of capacity to investigate and prosecute the crime means that criminal justice systems are often unable to meet the challenge of combating it. Beyond this, failure to secure smuggled migrants as witnesses means that prosecutions are often difficult and opportunities to convict are missed. Moreover, the smuggling of migrants is not always considered a serious crime for which a heavy penalty could be imposed. Ensuring that priority is given to investigating higher-level smugglers and taking due account of aggravating circumstances in the prosecution of cases involving the smuggling of migrants could have a deterrent effect on organised criminal groups. The underlying social, economic and political pressures that fuel the crime cannot be ignored. Unemployment, war and persecution are but three of the many reasons people decide to leave their home country. Pull factors include demand for cheap, undocumented labour in countries of destination. To better understand these dynamics and fully address the root causes of migration in order to prevent organized criminal groups from profiting from vulnerable groups such as migrants, a comprehensive response is required - one that involves examining the issues of migration and development

Smuggling of Goods

The sea is the circulatory system of the world economy, through which the economic blood of trade, ideas, and information flows. At odds with this healthy economic lifeblood are the pathogens of theft, corruption, and illicit trafficking.

In addition to patently illegal contraband, such as narcotics and weapons, numerous illicit goods move through the maritime transportation system, avoiding taxes and undermining legitimate trade. Tobacco is one of the most commonly smuggled illicit goods around the world. Next to it is narcotics. Heroin smuggling has been in the Asia Pacific region for years.

As Afghan heroin has become more important in local markets, a new crop of traffickers has entered the scene, including Nigerian and Pakistani groups. In Malaysia, for example, Pakistani networks are active. They use Malaysia as a hub to redistribute Afghan heroin to other countries in the region, including China and Australia[1]. In Indonesia, trafficking networks originating from India, Nepal, the Islamic Republic of Iran and Pakistan operate across the archipelago, particularly in Bali. Recent arrests indicate that international drug syndicates have recruited Cambodian, Indonesian and Thai nationals in place of the Iranians and Malaysians formerly used to smuggle heroin into Indonesia. In addition, West African criminal groups, particularly Nigerian groups, have increased their involvement in heroin trafficking though the region. According to the World Customs Organisation (WCO) only 2% of containers are checked in Ports and therefore, the tendency of large scale smuggling through ports are very likely.

Smuggling of Wildlife

In East Asia, population growth and burgeoning affluence have led to rising demand for exotic and luxury products, including wildlife products. China is both the region's largest economy and the largest consumer market for wildlife, imported for food, traditional medicinal ingredients, the pet trade, and exotic décor. A wide range of animal and plant products are imported, including those derived from protected species of bear, pangolin, reptiles, wildlife. Each of these products has a different trading chain, which may include domestic and international specialists involved in the storing, handling, transporting, manufacturing, marketing and retailing of wildlife. A number of techniques can be used to facilitate import, including the use of fraudulent paperwork and the mixing of protected species and lookalike species. Wildlife may also be "laundered" though exotic farms, zoos, and greenhouses – species harvested from the wild may be passed off as captive bred.

Illegal wildlife is often openly sold in otherwise legal market contexts. Prominent markets exist in Indonesia and the Philippines, while international border crossings between China and Thailand also function as wildlife markets. The growth of internet commerce has facilitated illicit trade in wildlife products. Given the number of species involved, it is almost impossible to come up with a clear estimate of the volume or value of the wildlife traded. It is apparent, however, that the trade in lesser-known animals such as pangolins is far greater in scale than that of large, emblematic species like tigers, pangolins or rhinos. The World Wide Fund for Nature - Malaysia (WWF-Malaysia) and The Wildlife Trade Monitoring Network (Traffic) have urged the Malaysian Government to act forcefully in combating poaching and wildlife trade in Malaysia[2]. Thailand used to be the number one in South East Asia but the country has recently come down hard on the trade, which estimated rakes in some RM61 billion a year. International smuggling doesn't only involve drugs and counterfeit goods. In fact, the illegal transport of wildlife parts has become one of the most lucrative forms of international crime. Black market demand has increased, threatening the future of the world's most magnificent animals. In the international market, smuggled horns are sold at a rate of USD 17,500 per pound to factories where they were carved into fake antiques or ground to powder for "possible medicinal purposes."

Illegal Fishing

Illegal, Unreported and Unregulated (IUU) fishing is a significant transnational crime problem that costs developing nations up to $15 billion in economic losses annually[3]. Perpetrators include established organized crime groups as well as commercial fishing operations; moreover the incidence of IUU fishing is often shaped and facilitated by corrupt public officials. Various economic drivers, the exceptionally high value of some species, and the Flag of Convenience (FOC) system of vessel registration contribute to the significance of the problem. Negative environmental impacts involve the depletion of fish stocks, damage to coral reefs, and stress on marine mammals and birds. Social and economic impacts are severe as well, and are most especially prevalent in developing nations. While an impressive number of initiatives, public and private, have been undertaken to address the problem, the very conditions that give rise to IUU fishing render attempts to combat the problem quite difficult. .

In addition to violations by commercial fishing operators, it is not uncommon for organized crime groups to engage in IUU fishing. In the 1990s Russian criminal syndicates were estimated to earn $4 billion a year through the illegal exportation of some two million metric tons of seafood, mostly Caspian Sea sturgeon and other seafood products to Japan, Europe, and the United States. Elsewhere, the illegal harvesting of abalone is thought to generate $80 million annually, and involves Russian syndicates,

Chinese Triads, and other Asian gangs. IUU fishing in South Africa is also associated with money laundering, drug trafficking, and racketeering. There has also been an observed overlap between IUU fishing and other forms of organised crime, including drug smuggling. Fishing vessels are integral to the transshipment of cocaine, activities which include the provision of offshore refueling services for ships carrying drugs, the transport of cocaine from larger ships to remote landing sites and commercial ports, and direct point-to-point delivery of cocaine shipments. Fishing vessels are also associated with the traffic in other types of illicit drugs, including heroin, marijuana, and amphetamines.

A significant link exists between IUU fishing and other forms of transnational organised crime, including trafficking in persons for the purpose of forced labor on fishing boats—a practice that includes the exploitation of women and children. De facto slavery in the fishing industry occurs across the world's oceans, but is especially prevalent off the coasts of West Africa and Southeast Asia[4]. Working conditions are often brutal, and include physical abuse, sexual exploitation, and in some cases, death. The principal actors in these human trafficking crimes are recruiters, senior crew on fishing vessels, and the fishing company or operator.

While it is widely agreed that IUU fishing is prodigious and global in scope, there exists substantial variability in the level and trend of IUU catches across regions. In a 2009 analysis of illegal and unreported catches in the territorial waters of fifty-four countries and fifteen high seas regions, researchers found that illicit activity was greatest in the Eastern Central Atlantic and least in the Southeast Asia[5]. Increased control by coastal states has led to a decline in illegal fishing in the Western Indian Ocean, while an increase in illicit activity in the Northwestern Pacific is due almost entirely to the role played by Chinese and Russian operators poorly policed by their home governments. Estimates of illegal and unreported catch in the Northeastern Pacific is low and continues to decline, but in the South east Asia the problem has been, and remains, relatively high, the waters about Indonesia are especially notorious as an area with a huge amount of unreported catch.

In many nations, coral reef ecosystem benefits many sectors including fisheries, tourism, and shoreline protection that are important to people's livelihoods, food security and well-being. As a result, threats to reefs not only endanger ecosystems and marine species, but also directly threaten the communities and nations that depend on them. The relative social and economic importance of reefs is further increased by the fact that many reef-dependent people live in poverty and have limited capacity to adapt to the effects of reef degradation.

According to the leading Non-Governmental Organisation (NGO), Tropical Research and Conservation Centre (TRACC)[6], illegal fishing consists of two types of operations, small-motorised boats which fish on an opportunistic basis in near shore waters for lobster, sea cucumber and fish, and larger live-aboard boats, which travel over very large distances. Most of these boats are fitted with hookah air compressors allowing diving to greater depths for cyanide fishing or increased exploitation of sea cucumbers living at greater depths. Local boats in areas with good fish populations search for fish by snorkeling, but most near shore, shallow reefs are so badly overfished and blasted by bomb fishing that there are few (if any) fish big enough to be wanted by the live fish trade. Boats which supply the live fish trade are equipped with a car tyre air compressor and two long, reinforced hoses for air delivery.

Piracy and Armed Robbery

The definitions of Piracy and Armed Robbery in accordance with UNCLOS & IMO are given in MSC.1/Circ.1333 & MSC.1/Circ.1334. Unlike most of the other organised crime problems, piracy is not a trafficking, smuggling or exploitation issue. No contraband is moved, no illicit market serviced and no marine resource is taken. Rather, it is a violent, crime which acquired goods by force. It is transnational because a ship is considered the sovereign territory of the nation whose flag she flies. It is organised because commandeering a ship at sea requires considerable planning and some specialised expertise, including information on goods they carry and passage times. The crime will be impossible without an organised crime network.

The term "piracy" normally encompasses two distinct sorts of offences: the first is robbery or hijacking, where the target of the attack is to steal a maritime vessel or its cargo; the second is kidnapping, where the vessel and crew are threatened until a ransom is paid. In the IORA region, Somali pirates had been active while now, the Gulf of Guinea and

South East Asia "petro-pirates" have been on the prowl. Concerted actions through public-private partnership should be put into action learning from countering Somali pirates.

Fueling Transnational Organised Crime (TOC) - Money Laundering

The term 'money laundering' allegedly originated in a scam set up by Al Capone in Chicago in the 1920s in which he set up a Chinese laundry through which he passed the profits of criminal activities in order to disguise their origins. The term money - laundering nowadays means precisely that: disguising the origins of money, so that the profits of, for example, illegal drugs sales cannot be traced back to their origins. For law enforcement agencies around the world the struggle against money laundering has become one of the focal points of the struggle against organised crime. The idea is that organised crime will find it increasingly difficult to operate if it cannot transfer its ill-gotten gains from the criminal underworld into the legal 'upper world'. From the standpoint of organised crime money laundering is an extremely important activity. Much money earned through crime remains, of course, within the criminal underworld. Some of the profits from one crime will simply be reinvested in other crimes.

International Measures to Address TOC

United Nations Office of Drugs and Crime (UNODC) has taken necessary steps[7]in addressing TOC. In combating a global phenomenon such as transnational organised crime, it advocates partnerships at all levels. Governments, businesses, civil society, international organisations and people in all corners of the world have a part to play. In the advisory, UNODC has noted some aspects that are critical in fighting organised crime which include:

(a) **Coordination**: Integrated action at the international level is crucial in identifying, investigating and prosecuting the people and groups behind these crimes.

(b) **Education and awareness-raising**: Ordinary citizens should learn more about organized crime and how it affects everyday lives. Express your concerns to policy and decision makers so that this truly global threat is considered by politicians to be a top priority among the public's major concerns. Consumers also have a key role to play: know what you are purchasing, do so ethically and make sure that you do not fuel organized crime.

(c) **Intelligence and technology**: Criminal justice systems and conventional law enforcement methods are often no match for powerful criminal networks. Better intelligence methods need to be developed through the training of more specialized law enforcement units, which should be equipped with state-of-the-art technology.

(d) **Assistance**: Developing countries need assistance in building their capacity to counter these threats. An important tool that can help with this is the United Nations Convention against Transnational Organised Crime, which has been ratified by 170 parties and provides a universal legal framework to help identify, deter and dismantle organised criminal groups.

It is evident that the government understands the all too familiar problems in combating TOC and therefore the need to operate in task groups and use AMLATFA to freeze assets. This only goes to show that the effort to deter and suppress TOC through concerted efforts is the key. However, these efforts cannot be one-off and be governed through separate actions. A wholesome policy which encompasses a Whole of Nation (WoN) has to be formulated with targets identified to deter and suppress TOC. A strategy can then be devised to put a system in place to harness coordinated and comprehensive approach using the tools available. What is needed is not just operations and legislation. To be effective, it is pertinent to consider the following:

(a) **Effective Prosecution**. Deploy full range of capabilities to collect enough evidence to stay ahead of crime, decide response quickly and be effective to incriminate perpetrators.

(b) **Target Supply Chain**. The systematic dismantling of the crime supply chain is a better option than concentrating too much on the statistics of arrests

(c) **Increase Costs**. Reduce the gap between legitimate economy and shadow economy. When cost is high, crime will not be lucrative.

To effect the above needs, a one-stop-centre is needed to harness information and coordinate response for effective incrimination. Whilst concerted land-sea actions are coordinated, the effort must be to identify those who fuel and feed from TOC. The main idea is to reduce the gap between legitimate economy and shadow economy by increasing cost to crime. These costs can be implied through freezing of assets and accounts to deter and suppress TOC thus breaking the logistics chain of crime. There are many benefits in using systems as management solutions on this issue. One of them is that it harnesses the integrated approach and factors information as it develops. it enables enforcement agencies to be at the right place with the right information to arrest the right criminal and through them, identify the master minds and kingpins. It also enables systems to trace the origins of the crime, the funding of it through technical support and trends analysis. These measures will surely benefit the collection of information in a single repository which can be shared with regional and international partners in the effort to break the logistics chain of crime.

Recommendations

It is recommended that a policy to realise the Whole of Nation (WoN) approach by using systems to harness and manage information may be adopted. The WoN system will comprise of law enforcement staff in a one-stop-centre to link with a multiple entities that will provide useful information to deter and disrupt TOC.

Conclusion

There are huge threats out there that we are all familiar with: illegal trafficking by sea of humans, goods (fuel/weapons/narcotics) and wildlife; illegal fishing; and sea robbery and piracy. The list goes on. All of these activities have one thing in common: they rob coastal states of their rights to grow, to become more prosperous, and to contribute to making the global system stronger. The activities of transnational criminal organisations in particular present a huge risk, because these sophisticated intelligence-driven criminal networks need to be enabled and protected ashore in order to be successful moving their contraband by sea or using the sea as a medium for the criminal activities. There is a need to protect our resources to regulate access to the fish protein that feeds our population, and to the marine ecosystem that brings tourists economy to raise our standards of living through investment and jobs.

TOC Syndicates spend vast sums of money analysing maritime security regimes in all countries, identifying and then exploiting vulnerabilities, including the corruption of officials in constabularies, customs agencies, ports, governments and industries. The net effect is billions in lost revenues that could have been spent on good governance, and on strengthening our national instruments of power, from defence, to transportation infrastructure, to education and healthcare.

That said, maritime security relationships and governance are always evolving, they are never perfect. New lessons are always being learned. Still, the threat will forever be there, unless some form of deterrence and suppression is built regionally. This leads us back to the fundamental question: what is the best mix of capabilities for any coastal nation to achieve persistent decision quality national domain awareness? They say charity begins at home, and so, it is at home that a new approach has to be envisaged through a policy intervention. When others can do it, so can we.

Notes

1   www.unodc.org

2   Ruben Sario (2013, Dec 17). *Crackdown on sale of wildlife meat.*Retrieved from The Star newspaper. Can be accessed via The Star Online: http://www.thestar.com.my/

3   Environmental Justice Foundation, "Pirates and Profiteers: How Pirate Fishing Fleets are Robbing People and Oceans, 2005, London

4   Liddick, Don, 'The dimensions of a transnational crime problem: the case of iuu fishing." *Trends in Organized Crime.*

5   Agnew, David J, John Pearce, GanapathirajuPramod, et al, "Estimating the Worldwide Extent of Illegal Fishing." *PloS one, 2009*

6   http://tracc-borneo.org/home/.

7   http://www.unodc.org/documents/toc/factsheets/TOC12_fs_general_EN_HIRES.pdf

Combating Maritime Crime and Legal Capacity Building

Stuart Kaye

Abstract

This chapter presents some of the challenges and responses for Combating maritime crime in the Indian Ocean region. It also presents a narrative about the legislative responses of different States, examples of cooperation and the scope for further cooperation.

Introduction

This chapter considers some of the issues and responses in the Combating of maritime crime in the Indian Ocean region. It considers factors such as geography, the complications of varying legal systems across the region, the impact of extra-regional States, and what responses might and have been possible.

Geography

The challenge of Combating maritime crime in the Indian Ocean Region is to no small extent affected by the geography of the region. The region itself is vast, but more significantly has very different littoral States around its extent, making cooperation and coordination of activities very difficult. The region can be divided into a number of different geographical sub-units where the maritime security issues and the importance of maritime trade are different. For example, looking at East Africa and around the Gulf and Arabian Peninsula, even within this sub-region the capacity and history of the littoral States is very different. There are emerging African economic powers in South Africa, Kenya and Tanzania, States with lesser economic capacity such as Mozambique, Madagascar and Comoros, the instability of Somalia, Iraq and Yemen, the great wealth of Saudi Arabia and the western Gulf States, as well as Iran. The maritime challenge for most is to make sure that there is safe transit from the Mediterranean into the Indian Ocean, although there are local security issues focused on piracy, illegal fishing and drug smuggling. In the Western Indian Ocean south of India there are different challenges. In the waters around the Maldives and Sri Lanka, and up into the Bay of Bengal, the security interests have a different focus, and are far more concerned with local security, and the assertion of jurisdiction over security-related matters. Finally, there are different issues for South East Asia. The important trade routes through the Indonesian archipelago, particularly the entrance to the Indian Ocean via the Straits of Malacca are very important, as they provide the principal route between the Indian and Pacific Oceans, which are vital to the trade of States such as Australia, China, Japan and the Republic of Korea. Ensuring that the Strait of Malacca remains open is essential, as well as local security issues, such as piracy and armed robbery at sea. Distilling these different interests into a common position presents a challenge to any State looking to develop an Indian Ocean approach to maritime security.

Legal Systems

In addition to these geographical areas, the region can be divided by virtue of its legal systems. A number of the States, particularly in the Western Indian Ocean are Commonwealth countries and make use of a system of law derived from the British common law. Examples include Tanzania, Kenya, Seychelles, South Africa and Mauritius, although there are still aspects of civil law in the cases of Mauritius and South Africa. Mozambique is also a Commonwealth country but draws its legal heritage from the Portuguese. Pakistan, India, Sri Lanka and the Maldives as well as Bangladesh, Malaysia and Australia also draw from the common law with respect to their legal heritage, and are members of the Commonwealth. These countries having a common background in law tend to rely upon territorial jurisdiction. Other States in the region draw their legal traditions from elsewhere but these tend to concentrate on the use of nationality jurisdiction based around the person to find the jurisdiction of competence. What this can mean is that States have different approach to how their criminal law is organized and applied to the citizens and other individuals. As a result this makes cooperation with respect to maritime applications of criminal law a little more difficult.

The different legal systems are only part of the problem. Many of the States in the region have not updated their maritime security and maritime crime legislation on a regular basis. In fact, many of the States still rely substantially upon criminal law that dates to colonial times. The McCauley Code which was introduced into India in the 1860s is still used in a slightly modified form in many commonwealth countries in Africa and South Asia. This presents a challenge because the kinds of maritime criminal responses that were needed in the 1860s and 70s are not those that are needed today. Some States have recognized this particularly those who face challenges to their maritime security. Kenya, for example, has substantially updated its legislation to ensure that it could better respond to the threats of piracy that have existed within the region. Malaysia did much the same thing at an earlier time with respect to coping with Straits of Malacca piracy. Similarly, India after arresting the *Alondra Rainbow*, felt that its piracy legislation was dated to the 19th century and in 2012 moved to update that legislation by introducing a bill to try to bring in contemporary reform. The most successful has been Mauritius which in 2013 substantially updated its maritime legislation. This legislation now is amongst the best in the region and perhaps is an example to others as to how to proceed.

These difficulties operate in a foundational level as can be shown in Fig. 1.

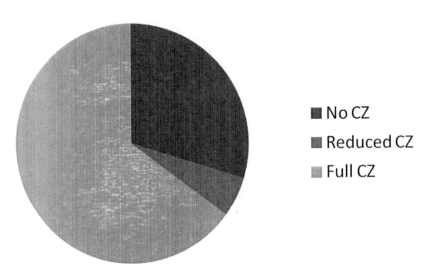

■ No CZ

■ Reduced CZ

■ Full CZ

Fig. 1. Indian Ocean Littoral States and Contiguous Zones (CZ)

Fig. 1 shows the application of a contiguous zone by States in the Indian Ocean region beyond the membership of IORA. What is apparent is that while two thirds of Indian Ocean States have proclaimed a contiguous zone, almost a third still do not, even though this is something that has been a clear right that they possessed in international law for many years. If a State does not have a contiguous zone then it is not making full use of the range of legal responses that can be applied in such a zone. Given the relevance of the customs jurisdiction applicable to the contiguous zone is the principal vehicle for drug and weapons smuggling offences, it means that the declaration of a contiguous zone is a relatively straightforward response for States to combat smuggling. The fact that almost one third of regional States have not availed themselves of such an uncontroversial action represents a puzzling omission. It shows that there is still work to be done in the region just to have the full range of legal responses that are needed.

Impact of Extra-Regional Players

Maritime security coordination in the Indian Ocean region is also complicated by the presence of a number of extra-regional players, who are deeply interested in the stability and safety of the region. Three of the States have a form of physical presence in the region. France still retains sovereignty over Reunion and Mayotte, as well as several small islands in the Southern Ocean and have contested claims to a number of other small features. Britain has retained sovereignty over the Chagos Archipelago, in the centre of the Indian Ocean, creating the British Indian Ocean Territory. This sovereignty is disputed by Mauritius, and has given rise to a series of disputes and an international arbitration. The Archipelago has been leased by Britain to the United States, who have developed a large military base on the atoll of Diego Garcia, and who have a substantial military presence in the heart of the region.

While these States manifest a permanent presence, they are by no means the only States with interests in the maritime security of the region. Very substantial volumes of seaborne trade pass through the region, as it provides the principal routes for petroleum leaving the Middle East, as well as trade between Europe, Indian sub-continent and Asia. As such, many extra-regional States have directly sought to engage in a variety of actions in the context of maritime security. Example include those States who participated in anti-piracy patrols of the Horn of Africa (Table 1), and the membership of Regional Cooperation Agreement on Combating Piracy and Armed Robbery against Ships in Asia (ReCAAP), which includes a range of extra-regional States including Brunei Darussalam, Cambodia, China, Denmark, Japan, the Republic of Korea, Laos, the Netherlands, Norway, the Philippines, Singapore, the United Kingdom, the United States and Viet Nam.

Table 1. States that participated in Anti-Piracy Patrols off the Horn of Africa

Australia	France	Malaysia	Saudi Arabia
Belgium	Germany	Netherlands	Spain
Bulgaria	Greece	New Zealand	Sweden
Canada	India	Pakistan	Thailand
China	Iran	Portugal	Turkey
Colombia	Italy	Romania	Ukraine
Denmark	Japan	Russia	United Kingdom
Finland	Korea, Rep. of	Singapore	United States

The presence of extra-regional players means that whatever solutions might be sought, States from outside the Indian Ocean will want "a seat at the table" in addition to those States from the region, as they will be of the view that the security of the Indian Ocean affects their vital interests as much as it affects those littoral States. When combined with the extraordinary variation of States within the region, makes coming together to cooperate over maritime security a tremendous challenge.

Responses

These difficulties do not mean that cooperation has been absent in the Indian Ocean Region. In fact, the region has been one of the more progressive areas of the world in addressing maritime security. It is fair to say though that what cooperation has existed has largely been issue-based. That is to say, where a problem is arisen, States have worked together to find a specific solution to respond to that problem. Good examples include those directed towards piracy, in both the east and west of the Indian Ocean. Joint piracy patrols and cooperative intelligence sharing has occurred to varying degrees, and this has helped to combat the rise of piracy. Sustained pressure through patrols and intelligence sharing saw levels of piracy fall in the waters of the Malacca Straits in the first decade of the 21st Century and in the waters around the Horn of Africa in the second decade.

While allowing for a more effective response in the short term, more specific cooperation might effectively limit the ability of regional States to be able to cooperate more widely. Some of this has been extra-regional or internally driven depending on the problem. So, where the responses of States with respect to piracy have led to tangible changes, these measures may not always be best suited for the kind of cooperation necessary to combat different types of criminal activity. However, where some cooperation has occurred, there is some prospect that it might provide a basis for wider discussions. Drug interdiction in the western Indian Ocean might be seen as an example of the transition of cooperation from piracy to other forms of crime. Extra-regionally, the adoption of the Djibouti Code to try to assist in the protection of vessels from piratical attack around the Horn of Africa is an example of cooperation, as is ReCAAP which was initiated now more than a decade ago with a focus on intelligence sharing. Another endeavour that has helped in this regard has been naval cooperation such as the Indian Ocean Naval Symposium (IONS) which provides for increased dialogue between navies to enhance cooperation. It does not itself create concrete examples of cooperation but it allows dialogue and the dialogue may lead to bilateral or multilateral examples.

IORA has been an increasing focus for maritime security cooperation, with strong support from the States chairing the Association: Australia, India and Indonesia. For example, the promotion of maritime security has been entirely consistent with Australian foreign, development and trade policies in the region. Australia's stated aim is reflected in paragraph 6 of the Perth Communiqué of 1 December 2013:

> *We wish to broaden and deepen efforts through IORA to bolster maritime security and safety, particularly in light of continued threats to maritime commerce, and freedom of the high seas, consistent with the UN Convention on the Law of the Seas (UNCLOS); as well as on the safety of sea farers. We look to the upcoming Indian Ocean Dialogue in India to explore, inter-alia, concrete options to enhance counter-piracy cooperation, including through improved maritime information-sharing arrangements and stronger national legal capacity and laws.*

71

Another mechanism that could be useful in fostering cooperation is Commonwealth extradition arrangements under the London Scheme. Those States which are members of the Commonwealth of Nations (Table 2) have a standing extradition arrangement allowing them to be able to transfer individuals who are charged with serious offences between the various members.

Table 2. Commonwealth Members with Indian Ocean Littorals

Australia	Mozambique
Bangladesh	Pakistan
India	Seychelles
Kenya	South Africa
Malaysia	Sri Lanka
Maldives	Tanzania
Mauritius	United Kingdom (BIOT)

While this appears most encouraging in dealing with maritime crime, there are limits on the use of the London Scheme. A typical example can be seen in the Extradition Act of the Seychelles. It extends extradition arrangements automatically to all Commonwealth States, and covers a large range of offences, including several that would be of direct relevance in dealing with maritime crime. The list of offences within the Seychelles legislation is reasonably typical, as appears to spring from a standard list used by the Government of the United Kingdom in its dealing with the State in the lead up to independence. The offences are:

- Murder

- Manslaughter

- An offence against the law relating to abortion

- Maliciously or wilfully wounding or inflicting grievous bodily harm

- Assault occasioning actual bodily harm

- Rape

- Unlawful sexual intercourse

- Indecent assault

- Procuring, or trafficking in person for immoral purposes

- Bigamy

- Kidnapping, abduction or false imprisonment or dealing in slaves

- Stealing, abandoning or exposing or unlawfully detaining a child

- Bribery

- Perjury or subornation of perjury or conspiring to obstruct or defeat the course of justice

- Arson

- An offence concerning counterfeit currency

- An offence against the law relating to forgery

- Stealing, embezzlement, fraudulent conversion, fraudulent false accounting, obtaining property or credit by false pretences, receiving stolen property or any other offence in respect of property involving fraud

- Burglary, housebreaking or any similar offence

- Robbery

- Blackmail or extortion by means of threats or by abuse of authority

- An offence against bankruptcy or company law

- Malicious or wilful damage to property

- Acts done with the intention of endangering vehicles, vessels or aircraft.

- An offence against the law relating to dangerous drugs or narcotics

- Piracy

- Revolt against authority of the master of a ship or the commander of an aircraft

- An offence relating to pollution of or endangering or damaging the environment

- Offences established under international conventions or agreement to which the requesting country or state or requested country or state and the Republic are parties

The list includes piracy, assault occasioning actual bodily harm, robbery, damage to property, acts to endanger vessels or aircraft, mutiny in the air or sea, people trafficking for immoral purposes, kidnapping, drug offences, pollution or environmental offences, and offences under international conventions to which both States are parties. There are restrictions relating to certain types of offence being subject to extradition, including trial in absentia, and double jeopardy. Similar lists of offences exist in the laws of Mauritius, Kenya and Tanzania.

Conclusions

So, what is the way forward? Strengthening legislative responses is a very good start. It is necessary because many regional States' legislation is often out of date as discussed above. Updating legislation in the same fashion as Mauritius did only a few years ago would be a good way forward. It would also be useful to strengthen institutional cooperation around extradition and also look at strengthening prisoner transfer arrangements, which can make widening extradition arrangements more palatable to domestic audiences. This can also allow States, be they flag State, port States or coastal States, to be able to better respond to the extraterritorial nature of maritime crime. For a coastal State, where individuals responsible for crimes cannot be apprehended at sea, there is the prospect of working with others to ultimately bring offenders to justice, through cooperation and extradition. It can also permit the prosecution of individuals within the region, with extra-regional support. The pirate prosecutions undertaken by Kenya, Mauritius and Seychelles, under agreements with the United States and the United Kingdom, saw significant numbers of prosecutions, with patrols, arrests and financial support from the extra-regional States. While this was facilitated by the universal nature of the crime of piracy, it perhaps demonstrated what can be accomplished with good cooperation. Data sharing too is very important. This can be done at a relatively low security level and be institutionalized without the necessity of a detailed full treaty. The model here can be best exemplified by what has been done with respect to ReCAAP. ReCAAP has been very effective in giving States information about maritime crime and pirate activity South East Asia and levels of piracy in South East Asia have been at historic lows in the years since ReCAAP was established.

In the wake of the growth of pirate activity in the western Indian Ocean through the first decade of this Century, it is remarkable at the fragmentary nature of the responses by littoral States to deal with piracy and maritime crime. Most are ill prepared to respond to dealing with criminal activity in their maritime approaches, with many still relying upon colonial era legislation. Given that virtually all of these States have been independent for over 40 years, this is an extraordinary state of affairs.

Ultimately, criminal activity taking place on the sea, or criminal activity using the sea as a means of entry into a coastal State, requires two things. First, it requires a coastal State to have its maritime jurisdiction in order, so it can successfully prosecute individuals who commit crimes at sea. Second, responding may also require a regional response, and therefore all littoral States in the western Indian Ocean will each need to address their legislation applicable offshore. Failure by one or more States to take such action could undermine the effectiveness of measures taken by others.

There is still much work to be done, and it is to be hoped that States will begin to take concerted efforts to improve their offshore legislation, as has been the case in States such as Mauritius and Kenya.

References

W-C. Chan, B. Wright & S. Yeo (eds), *Codification, Macaulay and the Indian Penal Code*, Ashgate (2011).

C.J. Colombos, *The International Law of the Sea* (Longman, 1968)

R. Herbert-Evans, "Countering Piracy, Trafficking and Terrorism: Ensuring maritime Security in the Indian Ocean" April 2012 < http://www.stimson.org/images/uploads/research-pdfs/Indian_Ocean_Rising_Chapter_2.pdf>.

M.S. McDougall & W.T. Burke, *The Public Order of the Oceans: A Contemporary International Law of the Sea* (New Haven, 1987)

Efthimios E. Mitropoulos, "Piracy: orchestrating the response" 3 February 2011 see <http://www.imo.org/mediacentre/secretarygeneral/speechesbythesecretarygeneral/pages/piracyactionplanlaunch.aspx>

Amber Ramsay, "Barriers to Prosecution: The Problem of Piracy" see <https://www.cimicweb.org/cmo/Piracy/Documents/CFC%20Anti-Piracy%20Thematic%20Reports/CFC_Anti-Piracy_Report_Prosecution_Aug_2011_FINAL.pdf>.

I.A. Shearer, "Problems of Jurisdiction and Law Enforcement against Delinquent Vessels" (1986) 35 *International and Comparative Law Quarterly* 320

United Nations, *Table of claims to maritime jurisdiction* <http://www.un.org/Depts/los/LEGISLATIONANDTREATIES/PDFFILES/table_summary_of_claims.pdf>

J.M. Van Dyke, "Balancing Navigational Freedom with Environmental and Security Concerns" (2003) *Colorado Journal of International Environmental Law and Policy* 19

Legal Frameworks for Combating IUU Fishing in Thailand

Somjade Kongrawd

Abstract

This chapter deals with the legal framework on maritime safety and security and focuses on three main points. Firstly, the specific maritime security and safety framework dealing with maritime threats in Thai waters, which would affect the IOR. Secondly, the efforts that Thailand has made and are taking with respect to the legal framework to combat IUU fishing are presented. The third aspect pertains to the lessons learnt from the case studies of Kunlun/Taishan, the IUU fishing vessel detained by Thailand for six months and an example of the cooperative and legal framework among countries, international organizations and domestic agencies. The chapter also identifies the lack of effective control of fishing vessels by some flag States and flag of convenience problems by allowing IUU fishing vessels to change their flags many times at ease, as well as the need to strengthen regional cooperation, as done in the Kunlun/Taishan incident, to address the problems of IUU fishing more effectively.

Introduction

Crime at sea, including piracy, human trafficking, illegal immigration, Illegal, Unreported and Unregulated (IUU) fishing, disaster and pollution of the marine environment, do not recognize national boundaries. It has actual or potential effect across national borders. Dealing with such maritime safety and security threats involves many aspects. One of the main factors is the legal framework which is the actual process of using the law and of governing it. According to the principle of law, the government and its officials and agents are accountable under the law. All actions that affect people's basic rights and civil liberties need a legal basis to justify the limitation of such rights and liberties. As the nation-state is a primary unit in the international system, it may also be bound by this principle. Thus, both international and domestic legal frameworks are required to deal with maritime threats and incidents at all levels; domestic, regional and global, in addition to providing cooperation and raising awareness.

For the purpose of this chapter I will present three main points. Firstly, the specific maritime security and safety framework dealing with maritime threats in Thai waters, which would affect the IOR. Secondly, the efforts that Thailand has made and are taking with respect to the legal framework to combat IUU fishing are presented. The third aspect pertains to the lessons learnt from the case studies of Kunlun/Taishan, the IUU fishing vessel detained by Thailand for six months and an example of the cooperative and legal framework among countries, international organizations and domestic agencies.

Legal Framework Dealing with Maritime Threats and Incidents for Maritime Safety and Security in Thailand[1]

Thailand has established the Thai Maritime Enforcement Coordinating Centre: Thai-MECC since January 1997. The centre has been the main mechanism to coordinate well over 30 agencies to deal with various challenges which arise at sea. However, its core operational unit comprises of six maritime agencies; namely the Royal Thai Navy, the Marine Police Division, the Customs Department, the Department of Fisheries, the Marine Department, and the Department of Marine and Coastal Resources. This structure renders the Centre ineffective due to the lack of unity of command. This is further exacerbated by the fact that the Centre has a coordinating, and not a commanding and controlling, function. In many instances each maritime agency's work is an unnecessary duplication or a fragment among them. In early 2005, the Cabinet approved a plan to upgrade the status of the MECC to maritime enforcement functions to handle security issues and to protect marine resources under the command of the Prime Minister. Currently, it is also responsible for IUU fishing, modern slave labour and human trafficking under the command of Command Center for Combating *Illegal Fishing* (CCCIF).[2] It is estimated that the new Thai-MECC will be established in October 2016 under a specific law. Thai-MECC classifies such maritime threats and incidents for maritime safety and security in Thailand into 9 types and has 9 major groups of legal frameworks. This section highlights the international and domestic law which makes up the legal framework governing the 9 group of maritime threats. The summary of this information can be found in Figure 1 of the Appendix.

1. **Piracy and Armed Robbery Against Ships.**

    (a)   International Law includes the United Nations Convention on the Law of the Sea, 1982 (UNCLOS) Articles 100-107; the Convention for the Suppression of Unlawful Acts against the Safety of Maritime Navigation (SUA Convention), 1988[3]; the Code of Practice for the Investigation of the Crimes of Piracy and Armed Robbery Against Ships (IMO Guidance and reports), adopted by IMO Resolution A.1025(26); and the Regional Cooperation Agreement on Combating Piracy and Armed Robbery Ships in Asia (ReCAAP), 2004.

    (b)   Domestic Law[4] governing the issue include the Prevention and Suppression of Piracy Act, B.E.2534 (1991) and the Criminal Code.

2. **IUU Fishing**

    (a)   The International Law dealing with IUU fishing is UNCLOS 1982, while the 1993 FAO Agreement to Promote Compliance with International Conservation and Management Measures by Fishing Vessels on the High Seas (FAO Compliance Agreement), the 1995 United Nations Conference on Straddling Fish Stocks and Highly Migratory Fish Stocks (UN Fish Stocks Agreement, 1995), the 1995 FAO Code of Conduct for Responsible Fisheries, the 2001 International Plan of Action to Prevent, Deter and Eliminate Illegal, Unreported and Unregulated Fishing (IPOA-IUU) and the 2009 Agreement on Port State Measures to Prevent, Deter and Eliminate Illegal, Unreported and Unregulated Fishing (PSM Agreement) are in the process of being included. As for regional fisheries management organizations, known as "RFMOs", these are considered the hub of management for fish stocks in various areas and provide the forum for countries to agree on conservation and management decisions, fishing allocations, including adoption, implement and enforcing measures to combat

IUU fishing. Thailand has also been a party to Indian Ocean Tuna Committee (IOTC).

(b)   Domestic Law includes the Fisheries Act B.E.2558 (2015),[5] Fisheries Right in Thai Water Act B.E.2482 (1949), National Council for Peace and Order (NCPO) Orders[6] No 10, 24 and 42 of 2558 (2015).

3.   Smuggling and Trafficking of Persons by Sea

(a)   The issue is governed by these International Laws; the United Nations Convention against Transnational Organized Crime, 2000; Protocol against the Illicit Manufacturing and Trafficking in Firearms, Their Parts and Components and Ammunitions, 2001; Protocol against the Smuggling of Migrants by Land, Sea and Air (The Migrants Protocol), 2004; Protocol to Prevent, Suppress and Punish Trafficking in Persons, especially Women and Children (The Trafficking in Persons Protocol), 2003; International Humanitarian Law and International Human Rights Law 1991 Convention and 1967 Protocol (Status of refugees and the principle of non-refoulement); and the Convention on Facilitation of International Maritime Traffic, 1965.

(b)   Domestic Law includes the Immigration Act B.E.2522 (1979); Anti-Trafficking in Persons Act B.E. 2551 (2008); Preventing and Suppressing Organized Crime B.E.2557 (2014)

4.   Illicit Traffic in Narcotic Drugs and Psychotropic Substances

(a)   International Law which governs the matter include the UNCLOS 1982, Article 108 and the United Nations Convention against Illicit Traffic in Narcotic Drugs and Psychotropic Substances 1988

(b)   The Domestic Law concerned are the Narcotics Control Act, B.E.2519 (1976); the Narcotics Act B.E.2522 (1979); the Psychotropic Substances Act, B.E. (Psychotropic Substances Act, B.E.2518 (1976); the Emergency Decree on the Prevention of the Use of Volatile Substances Act, B.E.2533 (1990); the Act on Measures for the Suppression of Offenders against the Laws relating to Narcotics B.E. 2534 (1991); the Money Laundering Prevention and Suppression Act (No. 2) B.E. 2551 (2008); the Special Case Investigation Act, B.E. 2547 (2004); the Drug Case Procedure Act, B.E. 2550 (2007); and the Custom Act B.E.2469 (1926).

5. Illicit Trafficking in Arms and Weapons of Mass Destruction

(a)　　International Law includes the Protocol against the Illicit Manufacturing of and Trafficking in Firearms, Their Parts and Components and Ammunition, supplementing the United Nations Convention against Transnational Organized Crime, 2001; UN Security council Resolution 1540; The Protocol of 2005 to the Convention for the Suppression of Unlawful Acts against the Safety of Maritime Navigation (2005 SUA Protocol)[7]; Convention on the Physical Protection of Nuclear Material,1980; Treaty on the Non-Proliferation of Nuclear Weapons, 1968; the Convention on the Prohibition of the Development, Production and Stockpiling of Bacteriological (Biological) and Toxin Weapons and on Their Destruction, 1975; and the Convention on the Prohibition of the Development, Production, Stockpiling and Use of Chemical Weapons and on their Destruction, 1993.

(b)　　Domestic Law includes Custom Act B.E.2469; Act on Navigation in Thai Waters, B.E. 2456 (1913) as amended until Act (No.15), B.E.2540 (1997); and the Act Authorizing the Navy to Suppress Some Crimes at Sea B.E.2490 (1947).

6. Intentional and Unlawful Damage to the Marine Environment

(a)　　International Law concerned are the United Nations Convention on the Law of the Sea, 1982 Part 12 Protection and Preservation of Marine Environment; Convention on the Prohibition of Military or Any Other Hostile Use of Environmental Modification Techniques, 1976; the International Convention for the Prevention of Pollution of the Sea by Oil, (OILPOL), 1954; the International Convention relating to Intervention on the High Seas in Cases of Oil Pollution Casualties (INTERVENTION), 1969; the International Convention for the Prevention of Pollution from Ships (MARPOL), 1973 Annex I-VI; Protocol of 1996 to the Convention on the Prevention of Marine Pollution by Dumping of Wastes and other matter, 1972; the International Convention on Oil Pollution Preparedness, Response and Co-operation (OPRC), 1990; the International Convention on the Control of Harmful Anti-Fouling Systems (ANTI-FOULING), 2001; and the International Convention for the Control and Management of Ships' Ballast Water and Sediments, 2004

(b)   Domestic Law includes the Act on Navigation in Thai Waters, B.E. 2456 (1913) as amended until Act (No.15), B.E.2540 (1997); the Thai Vessels Act, B.E. 2481 (1938) as amended until Act (No. 6), B.E. 2540 (1997); the Enhancement and Conservation of National Environmental Quality Act, B.E. 2535 (1992); the Marine Salvage Act, B.E. 2550 (2007); and the Fisheries Act B.E. 2558 (2015)[8].

7.   Maritime Terrorist

(a)   International Law framework involves the the United Nations Convention against Transnational Organized Crime, 2000; Protocol against the Illicit Manufacturing and Trafficking in Firearms; Convention for the Suppression of Unlawful Acts against the Safety of Maritime Navigation (SUA Convention), 1988; the Protocol of 2005 to the Convention for the Suppression of Unlawful Acts against the Safety of Maritime Navigation (2005 SUA Protocol); the Convention for the Safety of life at Sea (SOLAS), 1974and Protocol 1978 and 1988;the International Ship and Port Facility Security Code (ISPS Code), amended to SOLAS; and the ASEAN Convention on Counter Terrorism, 2007.

(b)   Domestic Law includes the Act on Offences Relating to Offshore Petroleum Production Places, B.E. 2530 (1987); and the Criminal Code Sections 135/1 to 135/5.

8.   Natural Disasters

(a)   International Law governing the issue includes the United Nations Convention on the Law of the Sea, 1982 Article 98(1); the International Convention on Maritime Search and Rescue (SAR), 1979; the International Convention for the Safety of Life at Sea, 1974 (SOLAS); and the ASEAN Regional Programme on Disaster Management-ARPDM.

(b)   Domestic Law includes the Disaster Prevention and Mitigation Act, B.E.2550 (2007); and Marine Salvage Act, B.E. 2550 (2007).

9. Marine Serious Incidents

(a)   International Law regulating the matter involve the United Nations Convention on the Law of the Sea, 1982 Part 12 Protection and Preservation of Marine Environment; the Convention on the Prohibition of Military or Any Other Hostile Use of Environmental Modification Techniques, 1976; the International Convention for the Prevention of Pollution of the Sea by Oil, (OILPOL), 1954; the International Convention relating to Intervention on the High Seas in Cases of Oil Pollution Casualties (INTERVENTION), 1969; the International Convention for the Prevention of Pollution from Ships (MARPOL), 1973 Annex I-VI; Protocol of 1996 to the Convention on the Prevention of Marine Pollution by Dumping of Wastes and other matter, 1972; the International Convention on Oil Pollution Preparedness, Response and Co-operation (OPRC), 1990; the International Convention on the Control of Harmful Anti-Fouling Systems (ANTI-FOULING), 2001; the International Convention for the Control and Management of Ships' Ballast Water and Sediments, 2004; the International Convention for the Safety of Life at Sea (SOLAS), 1974; the International Convention on Load Lines, 1966 and 1988 Protocol; and the Convention on the International Regulations for Preventing Collisions at Sea, 1972 (COLREG).

(b)   Domestic Law includes the Disaster Prevention and Mitigation Act, B.E.2550 (2007); The Enhancement and Conservation of National Environmental Quality Act, B.E. 2535 (1992); the Act on Navigation in Thai Waters, B.E. 2456 (1913) as amended until Act (No.15), B.E.2540 (1997); the Thai Vessels Act, B.E. 2481 (1938) as amended until Act (No. 6), B.E. 2540 (1997); and the Fisheries Act, B.E. 2558 (2015)[9].

Steps undertaken by Thailand on strengthening Legal framework to Combat IUU Fishing

Thailand, as a member State of the Indian Ocean Tuna Commission and the IOR, accepts the resolutions from the IOTC meeting and related resolutions.[10]   Unfortunately, The European Commission (EU) has issued a yellow card to Thailand for not taking sufficient measures in the international fight against IUU.[11] Thailand has taken many steps as follows to improve and develop fisheries management, including legislation of the new fisheries law.[12]

(a)   Reforming the legal framework to comply with international standards as the fisheries law had long been implemented since it came into force in B.E.2490 (1987) before the revising of Fisheries Act B.C.2558 (2015)

(b)   Most of the new Fisheries Act B.C.2558 (2015) provisions do not cover the IUU fishing issues. As a result, Thailand is drafting the new Fisheries Act.

(c)   The new fisheries law will provide a clear and coherent legal framework consistent with international law. It introduces a well-designed sanction scheme with serious penalties that will be effective in deterring IUU fishing activities. Thailand aims to submit the new fisheries law to the Cabinet by late October 2015[13].On 14th November 2015 such new law, namely, the Royal Ordinance on Fisheries came into force.

(d)   Future Ratification of the UN Fish Stocks Agreement and the FAO Port State Measure Agreement. As Thailand has not been a part of these Agreements it has to ratify them to fully enable the implementation of these provisions under the new Thai fisheries law urgently.

(e)   Having finished NPOA-IUU, the political commitment for combating IUU fishing, setting up the Center Command for Combating Illegal Fishing (CCCIF), rethinking fisheries management, improving Monitoring, Control and Surveillance (MCS), and ensuring traceability of fishing products is high.

Case Studies of Kunlun[14]/ Taishan: Cooperative and Legal Framework

Background

Kunlun is well known as an IUU vessel. It has changed its name, national registration ("flag") and other identifying characteristics several times to avoid the detection of prohibited fishing activities. By repeatedly changing these characteristics, the owners and operators wanted to avoid the sanctions associated with "blacklisting".

The Kunlun, a well-known IUU vessel, has been earlier named as Taishan, Chang Bai, Hongshui, Huang He 22, Sima Qian Baru 22, Galaxy, Dorita, Black Moon, Ina Maka and Corvus. It has used several flags but at that time it flew the flag of Equatorial Guinea and had earlier used flags of Indonesia, Tanzania, North Korea (DPRK), Panama, Sierra Leone, Equatorial Guinea, Saint Vincent and the Grenadines as well as of Uruguay.[15]

IUU Fishing Activities and Cooperative Framework Dealing with Taishan

Kunlun / Taishan was detected fishing illegally by a Royal New Zealand naval patrol vessel on 7 January 2015 at 070452Z in the Area regulated by the Convention on the Conservation of Antarctic Marine Living Resources (CCAMLR). At the time the Kunlun was hauling gill nets laden with tooth fish. Gill netting is a prohibited fishing method within CCAMLR. When approached by the patrol vessel, the Kunlun continued to fish and did not give any indication that the vessel would cease fishing and leave the area.[16]

According to the markings on the stern of the Kunlun, the flag being flown and information provided by the master of the vessel, it was registered in Equatorial Guinea. New Zealand sought clarification from the Government of Equatorial Guinea regarding the flag status of the Kunlun. Equatorial Guinea stated that it had no registered vessels in the CCAMLR Area and authorised New Zealand to board the Kunlun. But it occurred in the CCAMLR Area, which is High Sea Area and Equatorial Guinea is not a CCMLR member country. As a result, it lacked legal basis to board, arrest and seize the vessel.

On the 14th of January 2015, an attempt was made to board the Kunlun but the vessel evaded the New Zealand patrol vessel by steaming away at high speed into a hazardous sea ice area. Later, on the 27th of February 2015, the Kunlun was boarded by an Australian patrol vessel who conducted a flag state verification. The master of the Kunlun claimed the vessel was flagged to Equatorial Guinea.

On the 6th of March 2015, the Kunlun entered the port of Phuket, Thailand, claiming to be the Taishan and flagged to Indonesia. The catch on board was declared to Thai authorities as grouper and was unloaded into containers for transportation to the port of Songkhla, Thailand for embarkation on a merchant vessel bound for Vietnam. Thai authorities intercepted the containers and inspected the contents, confirming that the fish had been falsely declared as grouper when in fact it was tooth fish. A fine was imposed for this false declaration and subsequent enquiries by Thai authorities with Indonesia confirmed that the vessel was not flagged to that country. As a result, Thailand considered Taishan as a stateless vessel, and asked for real nationality and other IMO safety documents. If Taishan did not submit the documents, the marine department would not issue port clearance documents for it to depart the port. The custom department fined the exhibited fish separately, as false declaration of fish species, according to the Custom Law Section 99 as faulty declaration at 500,000 THB (approximately 14,000 USD) and also under Section 138 as incorrect vessel reporting at 1,000THB (approximately 28 USD);

The Kunlun/Taishan was detained at about one nautical mile away outside the port of Phuket until 7 September 2015 when it was found that the vessel had steamed out of port at night without approval from Thai authorities. The Kunlun/Taishan is believed to be operating with a skeleton crew of about 5 persons and it is possible that it may have changed its name after departing Phuket. The destination of the Kunlun/Taishan is unknown but it is possible that it may be steaming to Cabo Verde to link up with associated IUU vessels, the Songhua and the Yongding. Both vessels have recently undergone a refit in Cabo Verde.

Lessons Learnt from Cooperative and Legal Framework

Although Taishan fled from the authorities without neither port clearancenor IMO safety documents, flag registered document included, the Thai Maritime Coordinating Centre (TMCC) comprising of Royal

Thai Navy, Maritime Department, Customs Department, Marine and Fisheries Department, Department of Marine and Coastal Resources with the cooperation of Immigration Bureau, local police and INTERPOL[17], Australian Fisheries Management Authority, Australian Customs and Border Protection Services, Indian Ocean Tuna Commission[18] fully cooperated with the agencies of other states and the Thai authorities in the investigation and sharing of information related to the vessel, resulting in penalties and it being detained for over six months.

Every time authorities disrupt an operator's plans, or interrupt the sale of catch when an IUU vessel is detained in port, or diminish the operator's profits by making the vessels sail further before they can find a port where they can offload their catch, it makes returning to the Southern Ocean to fish less economical. Therefore the actions taken by the Thai cooperative agencies will send a clear message that IUU operators are not welcome in Thai ports. These actions, along with those taken by other international partners, will help put operators, who are plundering an otherwise well-managed fish stock in the Southern Ocean, out of business for good. The result would be fewer IUU vessels in the Southern Ocean, Including Indian Ocean in the upcoming season.

Conclusion

Thailand's legal frameworks for dealing with maritime threats and incidents in Thailand are working well. However, it may need to be a party to international treaties like the SUA Convention, SAR Convention, UN Fish Stock, FAO Compliance Agreement, PSM Agreement and other RFMOs Agreement rather than IOTC in order to strengthen Thai law enforcement procedures for combating IUU fishing and other maritime threats and incidents. These will enhance the safety and security in the IOR.

As per IUU fishing problems, Thailand's legal framework for IUU fishing will fully cover all IUU standards very soon, with the provisions of strengthening the domestic laws to deal with stateless vessel like Taishan, both in port or High Sea, to arrest and to seize IUU vessels and IUU fish product or fine them at about thirty million Thai Baht.[19] Taishan's detention is the longest IUU vessel detention in the world which has set a good example in cooperation for deterring IUU fishing in CCMLR and nearby areas. However, more legal frameworks are required at all levels; domestic, regional and global which should include the effective control of fishing vessels by flag states. There is also a need to strengthen regional cooperation to address the problems of IUU fishing more effectively.

Notes

1   Office of the Judge Advocate General of the Royal Thai Navy, available at http://www.judge.navy.mi.th/main.html

2   CCCIF was established by the National Council for Peace and Order (NCPO). NCOP as a sovereignty can make laws concerning anything.

3   Thailand has not been parties both SUA Convention and Protocol 1988 and 2005. However, it is in the process of being a party for SUA 1988.

4   Council of State, available at http://www.krisdika.go.th/wps/portal/general/!ut/p/c4/04_SB8K8xLLM9MSSzPy8xBz9CP0os3g_A2czQ0cTQ89ApyAnA0__EIOAQGdXAwNDc_2CbEdFAIO8diA!/

5   It has been cancelled by the Royal Ordinance on Fisheries B.E. 2558 (2015) as its provisions do not cover the IUU matters. The Royal Ordinance entered in to forces on 14th November 2015.

6   NCOP as a sovereignty can make laws concerning anything.

7   Thailand has not been a party to 2005 SUA Protocol.

8   It has been replaced by the Royal Ordinance on Fisheries B.E. 2558 (2015) which came in to forces on 14th November 2015.

9   Ibid.

10 http://www.iotc.org/sites/default/files/documents/2015/10/IOTC-2015-WPDCS11-INF05_-_Thailand_NPOA_IUU.pdf

11 European Commission, Press release, available at http://europa.eu/rapid/press-release_IP-15-4806_en.htm

12 Royal Thai Embassy, Madrid, Spain. Highlights on Thailand's Effort to Combat IUU Fishing (24 August 2015), available at http://www.thaiembassy.org/madrid/contents/files/services-20150827-204219-928025.pdf.

13 Currently, it has been finished, namely the Royal Ordinance; entered in to forces on 14th November 2015.

14 COMBINED IUU VESSEL LIST available at http://iuu-vessels.org/iuu/iuu/search.

15 European Union law European Union law European Law, available at http://eur-lex.europa.eu/legal-content/EN/TXT/?uri=uriserv:OJ.L_.2015.199.01.0012.01.ENG

16 INTERPOL, Purple Notices No 248, available at http://www.interpol.int/INTERPOL-expertise/Notices/Purple-notices-%E2%80%93-public-versions

17 INTERPOL PURPLE NOTICE on 13/01/2015, 21/01/2015, 13/01/2015 and on 25/11/2015.

18 Indian Ocean Tuna Commission, IOTC CIRCULAR 2015-004, 16 January 2015.

19 Currently, it has been finished as mentioned earlier.

20 Available at http://www.judge.navy.mi.th/page-articles.html

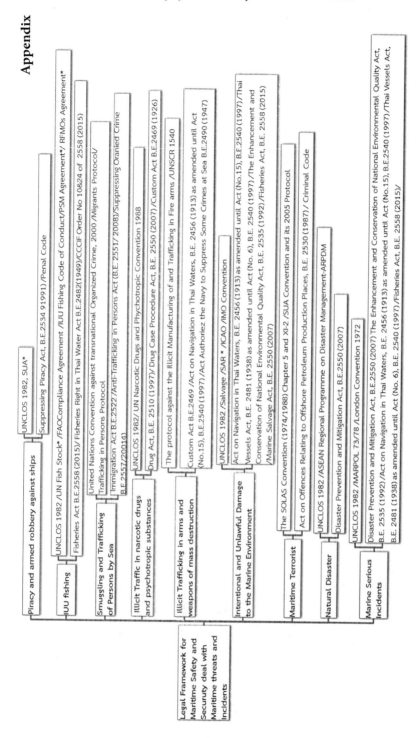

Figure 1: Legal Framework Dealing with Maritime Threats and Incidents for Maritime Safety and Security in Thailand[20]

Capability Building in the Indian Ocean Region

Anil Jai Singh

Abstract

The shift in the global geopolitical centre of gravity to Asia has led to attention being focussed on the Indian Ocean in an increasingly maritime-centric world characterised by globalisation, connectivity and the great movement of trade and energy across geographies. This has also spawned a multitude of traditional and non-traditional threats and challenges in the maritime domain which need to be addressed effectively from within. This region is fraught with uncertainties of different kinds and does not inspire much capacity or capability building either individually or collectively. However the threat is real and immediate thus making it imperative for a collaborative effort to be initiated sooner rather than later by nations through institutionalised and empowered mechanisms for any meaningful capacity building to address these threats and challenges. This chapter suggests various measures that can be initiated beginning from the "low hanging fruit" with incremental enhancement as greater mutual trust and confidence develops.

Introduction

The defining feature of the 21ˢᵗ century has been the shift in the global geopolitical centre of gravity to Asia and the evolving regional dynamics will ensure that it remains so for the foreseeable future. Globalisation, connectivity and the consequent economic interdependence in the movement of goods over the sea has ensured that the focus will be on a strong maritime orientation, thus placing the Indian Ocean specifically and perhaps in a larger geopolitical context, the Indo-Pacific at centre stage. The need for smooth flow of maritime trade is critical for most economies in this region. Effective management of these wide commons thus becomes

91

an existential imperative for many.

The Indian Ocean has many unique characteristics which differentiate it from the larger Atlantic and Pacific Oceans and further highlight the attention it deserves. Perhaps the single most important characteristic is that it is bounded by prominent choke points, each of which is critical to global trade and therefore vulnerable to disruptive forces pressing for their narrow and often unattainable objectives through coercive pressure which basically amounts to plain and simple blackmail. The Indian Ocean connects the Atlantic and Pacific Oceans and is the main waterway for the movement of global trade. On an average more than 110,000 ships transit the Indian Ocean annually with the Malacca Straits as one of five choke points bordering the Indian Ocean alone accounting for over 60,000 of these. The blocking of any choke point could therefore have a debilitating effect on the global economy.

The Maritime Threat

The nature of the maritime threat has also seen the emergence of a new paradigm with classic naval conflict (the raison d'etre of naval forces) sharing space with a sub-conventional, non-traditional hybrid construct which transcends geographical and political boundaries and poses a threat to the economic well-being of an increasingly connected world. The effect of Somali piracy, considered a low-intensity maritime threat in the spectrum of naval conflict, and restricted mostly to a limited area in an economically backward region of the world, underlined this as it took a sustained operation by global navies to contain this menace, a response that was totally disproportionate to the capacity and capability of the perpetrators. It is this asymmetry that defines the vulnerability of the Indian Ocean and the region as a whole. Even though the prominence of the Indian Ocean in the "Asian century" has created a series of security challenges which affect the world, the solutions to these have to be found from within.

This paradigm also extends to the non-military challenges to overall maritime security which has an impact on the societal, political and economic well-being of nations. Climate change and its effects are one example. Climate change alone has seen a sharp increase in humanitarian disasters through natural calamities which are increasing in both, frequency and intensity. The IOR seems particularly vulnerable to these with most nations lacking the basic capacity to address either the causes or the consequences. The rising sea levels are threatening the very existence of countries in this region and while a lot is being spoken and promised across multilateral and international organisations (Rio 2012, COP 21 etc.), precious little is being implemented. It would be naïve to assume that this issue, so intrinsic to our region will find external solutions – the nations of the IOR will have to address this from within. The competition for dwindling resources within and across the Indian Ocean is also likely to intensify. This could give rise to hegemonistic tendencies as is being witnessed in the South China Sea and through subtler means has started to become evident in the IOR as well. As the world turns towards the oceans to seek means of sustenance, nations will seek to dominate the global commons – the inherent weaknesses of the Indian Ocean littoral nations will provide extra-regional powers the opportunity to exploit the resource base essential for sustenance of this region which contains over 40% of the global population.

The Challenge Within

The sheer range of threats to maritime security therefore requires a regional multilateral cooperative approach based on mutual trust and a shared interest for the common good. The IOR however is characterised by political instability, internecine conflict, virulent nuclear rhetoric, terrorism by non-state, state sponsored and state actors, the spectre of failed and failing states, long standing bilateral and regional disputes and conflicts besides the presence of extra-regional powers pushing their own agenda by exploiting the inherent weakness and vulnerability of nations. A classic case is the destabilisation being caused due to the West driven regime change in West Asia leading to even greater chaos. All this and more further underlines the magnitude of the challenge to providing effective maritime security. The absence of an acceptable regional security framework presents an additional vulnerability. The Indian Ocean region must identify more areas of convergence, consolidate these and then leverage the confidence this generates to address the areas of divergence. This will require a great deal of patience, tenacity and focus – attributes not generally associated with the political ethos in this region.

Collaborative Capacity Building

One of the ways to move forward would be to address the challenges through a collaborative and consensual approach whereby each nation is mandated to develop its own capacity and capability commensurate with its size and stake in the region towards common capacity building. A non-confrontational construct can be established to provide HADR and SAR which does not threaten the countries. This can also address one of the region's vulnerabilities emanating from the lack of a cohesive regional identity amongst the Indian Ocean littoral states which in fact remain largely disaggregated with numerous regional sub-entities. This leads to bilateral and multilateral trust deficits extending very often to outright hostility and therein perhaps lies the region's greatest weakness. India and Pakistan– two significant IOR countries cannot see eye-to-eye on anything; SAARC, a grouping of South Asian neighbours has a host of issues afflicting it; there is the Shia-Sunni divide exacerbating the situation between Saudi Arabia and Iran, two major West Asian countries and threatening to spill over across a much larger geographical region. These are just a few.

A shared understanding and a committed approach with adequate institutionalised oversight and specific milestones will be the only way to ensure that the total is larger than the sum of its parts.

IORA – Bridging the Gap

The IORA is primarily a non – military construct with maritime security being a recent addition. This is a welcome step as security is now intrinsic in any economic construct. In its capacity as the overarching institutionalised political mechanism in the Indian Ocean, IORA's mandate should also include establishing an appropriate architecture to enhance the requisite capacity and capability for tackling at least those challenges which are non-military in nature but still have an impact on the overall security of the Indian Ocean region. It is in fact these vulnerabilities which expose this region to more death and destruction than a traditional security threat.

Traditional security issues are not easy to reconcile amongst nations and they being essentially sovereign in nature, convergences are hard to come by even in cases where collective security may be under strain. NATO, which is essentially a security alliance and successfully overcame the Soviet threat, is also finding itself under strain in the absence of a well-defined common adversary. Even ASEAN, a fairly successful and mature economic grouping is under strain despite being far smaller and more cohesive. China has successfully exposed its underlying vulnerabilities. Additional constructs like the ARF and the ADMM+ have to step in to address these challenges from a security perspective. Their effectiveness though is yet to be seriously tested.

The key to effective capacity and capability building lies in leveraging the strengths exhibited so far and identifying the weaknesses. The humanitarian relief after the tsunami of 2004, the search for the Malaysian airliner MH 370 and the combating of piracy in the western Indian Ocean may provide valuable lessons. In each of these an extra-regional initiative dominated whereas it should have been driven by an effective internal capability supported by extra-regional forces where required. It is this capacity building that needs to be established.

Recommendations

The important areas for capability and capacity building through a collaborative sharing of responsibility that could be initiated in the near and medium term are as follows:-

(a) Identifying the common threats like piracy, transnational crime and natural disasters and developing mechanisms to address these. Establish "expert" groups across various streams to offer recommendations on risk management, deconflicting issues of disconsonance, conflict resolution, peacekeeping, disaster management etc.

(b) Initiating 'Blue Economy' initiatives and addressing various issues related to sustainable development. Providing a collective voice on the subject at the UNO and other international bodies to ensure that it is heard and acted upon. The spectre of inundation of some island countries in the region will be upon us sooner than we expect and a reactive approach would be of little avail at that time.

(c) Robust Track 1.5 and Track 2 initiatives such as conferences and workshops to improve the general understanding of issues and address seemingly intractable disputes. This could effectively offer a way ahead for Track 1 initiatives. The ARF, ADMM+ and CSCAP model could be a good reference. However these need to be more than just talk shops and it will be for the governments to take these seriously.

(d) Confidence Building Measures to ensure transparency and allay mutual suspicions.

(e) Establishing comprehensive regional security architecture to address non-traditional threats also like environmental protection and climate change which threatens food, energy and resource security besides the demographic challenge like the recent refugee crisis in Europe. This will not be restricted to maritime issues alone but will also address sustainable development of coastal communities and ensure law-enforcement afloat and ashore.

(f) An exponential increase in dependence on ocean resources is going to become a source of disconsonance amongst nations with a real potential for conflict. Creation of a common trading arrangement with mutual FTAs could mitigate this eventuality as it would be of benefit to all.

(g) A collective responsibility towards SLOC and choke point security based on shared economic interests and interdependence and the imperative of safety of navigation on the wide commons.

(h) Maritime Domain Awareness and situational awareness information sharing mechanisms amongst maritime forces through a common grid through regional information sharing centres and a central data collection and dissemination centre including air space management.

(i) Strengthening of the coastal security architecture by nations to achieve a seamless coverage across maritime boundaries.

(j) Consolidation of existing bilateral and multilateral arrangements and promulgating protocols and SOPs towards enhancing sub regional interoperability and as the mechanism evolves and matures, towards regional interoperability.

(k) A permanent HQ with proportional representation by all stakeholders in a country and sector sharing format. This would centrally coordinate the activities, avoid duplication of effort and become the operational hub.

(l)   Allocation of forces and exercising them with periodic work-ups. These could be a combination of grey and white hulls as well as a rapid reaction element. This will also reduce the existing suspicions and contribute towards mutual confidence building.

(m) Leveraging the strengths of extra regional stakeholders in an inclusive economic and security architecture. Countries like the US and China are going to be in this region with considerable stakes – the Maritime Silk Road is one such. Leveraging the AIIB and the Silk Road Fund to build capacity and capability without compromising regional autonomy.

(n)   Retaining the autonomy of decision making on issues affecting this region. Anti-piracy was largely driven by the West because we did not have an institutional mechanism to do so. At best therefore we were a part of the process and not driving it.

(o)   Leveraging the complementarity of IORA and the Indian Ocean Naval Symposium (IONS) for military and constabulary functions. While IORA takes the lead in providing the political direction and shaping policy, IONS could translate that into creating a suitable response mechanism. IONS offers the correct platform to provide the operational appreciation, define the rules of engagement and shape the response etc. aligned with the political directive from IORA which will provide the legal and legislative authority. It will of course require considerable effort to get the desired convergence from the political and diplomatic establishment.

(p)   At a Navy, Coast guard and maritime security force level, greater engagement through increased participation in defence courses by member countries to build relationships and offer an external perspective. This can be at various levels – basic training, specialisation, Staff College and NDC.

(q)   Ship visits to each other's ports and exercises such as MILAN aimed primarily at developing a comprehensive understanding on convergent and divergent issues in a quasi-military framework while enhancing interaction at an individual level through social, cultural and sporting exchanges. MILAN has grown from a five nation exercise to a 17 nation exercise in less than two decades.

Events like the International Fleet review in Visakhapatnam, India provide an excellent platform.

(r) A collective voice in international forums towards addressing the regional environmental and security concerns. The IORA should create favourable conditions and encourage an increase in its membership. This will also give it a larger presence in world bodies.

(s) Capacity building through enhancing the defence industrial cooperation amongst the countries in the region. This will not only enhance the regional industrial base and improve technology induction into the region but will also mitigate the vulnerability created by sanction regimes initiated by external powers. It will also enhance diplomatic, economic and political commonalities.

Conclusion

Credible and effective capacity building and capability development is a major task in terms of time, money, people and resources and even more so perhaps in as disparate a grouping as the IOR littoral. However there is no getting away from it and therefore it is critical that the IOR begins addressing these issues sooner rather than later. It would perhaps be best to do so in a phased manner with the lower end of the spectrum or the "low hanging fruit" as a start and build incrementally as greater confidence and experience is gained. It should be seen as a long term investment in an increasingly fractious world and will require a sincere effort by nations to rise above bilateral and self-centred concerns in understanding the common "securonomic" issues posed to the region and to themselves and create a robust organisation to address these collectively.

Concluding Thoughts and Salient Recommendations

Gurpreet S Khurana

The structure and content of the one-and-half day Indian Ocean Rim Association (IORA) meeting of experts on maritime safety and security were tailored to draw upon the shared experiences of the member States in meeting their maritime interests while maintaining good order at sea, while also build upon the progress achieved in earlier meetings. Of the twenty IORA member States, fourteen were represented and a total of twenty-seven foreign and Indian delegates participated as speakers and chairpersons. In addition, there were representations from the New Delhi-based diplomatic missions of France, Seychelles, Thailand and the United States of America.

The key issues discussed during the meeting and the major findings may be broadly sub-divided into maritime safety and security 'challenges' and 'responses' for the countries of the Indian Ocean Region. These issues and findings, along with the salient takeaways from the meeting are stated below.

Challenges

The perspectives presented by delegates from various IOR countries indicated that although traditional military threats do exist, the predominant insecurities at sea emanate from non-traditional threats. The regional countries have prioritized their security concerns based on their own assessments of risk and vulnerability. The common non-traditional security threats to States include piracy, organized crime, Illegal, Unregulated and Unreported (IUU) fishing, and the challenges to human security, including those posed by natural phenomena. However, challenges such as illegal immigration, environmental degradation, and ill effects of climate change – such as rising sea levels – affect certain States more than others.

There were divergent perspectives amongst the delegates on the legitimacy, role and requirement of Private Maritime Security Companies (PMSCs). For example, while the delegates from Malaysia and Singapore supported the employment of PMSCs, the delegate from Madagascar did not, even stating that such practice could potentially encourage maritime terrorism.

The legal dimension is another challenge for the regional countries. It includes the existing voids in international law, and some countries not being parties to the international conventions. Further, some countries have not yet implemented the provisions of international law through domestic legislations, which is a cause of concern.

Many IORA member States are beset by significant constraints in terms of the capacity of maritime forces. This has led the regional countries to 'free-ride' on the maritime safety and security provided by extra-regional stakeholders. Such an approach is unavoidable, and is likely to continue into the foreseeable future. However, it has geopolitical pitfalls over the longer term. There is also a need to factor the geo-political friction among regional countries due to their differing approaches to maritime safety and security.

Responses

The delegates displayed much keenness to search for 'regional solutions' to maritime safety and security challenges in a manner that regional cooperation becomes a habit, rather than being limited to being an ad-hoc process.

Information-sharing was ascertained to be among the key facets of cooperation as per the 'least common denominator' approach. To counter organised crime at sea, the use of information-technology ('digital solutions') against the criminals on land was discussed as an important supplement to the response measures taken by maritime forces.

Some delegates recommended that the IORA emulate best practices of the ASEAN, such as the harmonisation of aeronautical and maritime

SAR. However, some members from the western Indian Ocean countries – such in Africa/ West Asia – were not amenable to do so, and preferred a sub-regional approach.

While sub-regionalism within IORA was discussed as necessary for cooperation on maritime safety and security, the delegates were agreeable to the IORA leading the collective approach of IOR countries at international fora.

The IORA needs to work closely with the Indian Ocean Naval Symposium (IONS). The IONS has already covered much ground since its inception in 2008 in terms of Information Sharing, Anti-Piracy operations and Humanitarian Assistance and Disaster Relief (HADR) missions. The IONS could effectively supplement the policies of the member States governments 'in the field' through capacity building of regional maritime forces and developing operational compatibility among the forces.

The Indian Ocean Dialogue (IOD) was accepted as a valuable bridge, not only between Track 1 and Track 2, but also between public and private stakeholders, and also as a forum to involve extra-regional stakeholders for regional capacity building. However, since IOD is a forum, where all issues pertaining to IORA charter are deliberated upon, the IORA would need a dedicated Core Group for Maritime Safety and Security. The Core Group could partner with the IONS, the Djbouti Code of Conduct (COC), and so on.

To achieve 'maritime safety and security' in the IOR, the IORA would need to adopt an 'inclusive' approach to security, which also involves the extra-regional stakeholders. The underlying imperative for this lies not only in the fact that the IOR countries lack adequate capacity and resources to fend for themselves, but the larger reality that any multilateral forum that excludes relevant stakeholders may become irrelevant itself. Besides, the existing inadequacies, imperfections and distortions in terms of international legal frameworks need to be seen from the global, rather than a regional perspective. However, IORA needs to develop into a cogent and cohesive multilateral forum through formulation of frameworks, parameters and norms. It should be strong and capable of effectively managing the behaviour of extra-regional stakeholders, and prevent any major-power rivalry that may emerge.

Recommendations

The Chairpersons of the five sessions were requested to give recommendations pertaining to their respective sessions. In the Concluding Session, a consensus was achieved on each point, by *in-situ* edits to the text of recommendations based on the inputs/ disagreements of the various delegates. The session-wise Chairpersons' recommendations are enumerated below.

> **Maritime Safety and Security: Regional Challenges**

- IORA members to establish national Point of Contact (PoC) for information-sharing and capacity building.

- Harmonize functioning of existing regional maritime safety and security organisations within IORA.

- Identify areas of overlap to de-conflict activities & optimize resource employment.

- IORA members to collectively articulate national positions at international fora.

> **Cooperative Organisational Structures in the IOR**

- Create a cooperative mechanism for sustainable development of marine resources.

- Encourage extra-regional stakeholders to engage IOR countries at sub-regional level for maritime Capacity Building, including in port security, disaster management & SAR.

- Explore collaborative ventures with other regional/ sub-regional organisations in the IOR.

- Consider global best practices in maritime safety & security.

- Strengthen Indian Ocean Dialogue (IOD) as a Track 1.5 mechanism for IORA.

> **Inclusive Approach to Maritime Safety and Security**

- Adopt inclusive approaches and strategies for maritime safety and security in the Indian Ocean Region (IOR).

- The approach should facilitate an effective and a comprehensive inclusive safety and security framework.

- Establish an IORA Maritime Safety and Security Core Group instead of an Indian Ocean Forum for maritime crime.

- Explore partnership between IORA and existing Maritime Safety & Security forums like IONS and IMO Djibouti Code of Conduct.

- Strengthen implementation of the Indian Ocean MOU on Port State Control (PSC) as instrument for maritime safety programme.

- Integrate national civil and military partnership for enhancing maritime safety and security.

➢ Legal Frameworks

- Member States are encouraged to join primary and secondary international treaties, with reservations/ statements, as necessary.

- Establish IORA mechanism for dispute resolution.

- Forge links with relevant international organisations such as IMO, among others, pertaining to legal issues of maritime safety and security.

- IORA members to update their domestic laws on maritime & criminal aspects.

- Evolve consensus on legal frameworks for PMSCs, info-sharing and maritime surveillance.

- Undertake legal capacity building through existing sub-regional arrangements, particularly for criminal jurisdiction.

➢ Capability Building and Capacity Optimization

- Insulate cooperation against non-traditional threats from geopolitics.

- Enhance frequency of regional maritime exercises involving both the navies and coast guards.

- Identify complementarities between IORA and IONS.

- Consider an inter-agency maritime task force based on common SOPs.

- Leverage capabilities of extra-regional stakeholders for capacity building of IORA member states.

- At national level, coordinate maritime security approaches among government agencies, port authorities and various industries like shipping, fishing, and oil and gas.

These recommendations were carried forward to the 16th Committee of Senior Officials (CSOs) meeting of the IORA for enhancing maritime safety and security in the Indian Ocean Region.

A Primer on Indian Ocean Rim Association (IORA)

The Indian Ocean Rim is a region comprised of the states whose shores border the Indian Ocean. The region is home to about two billion people. It is a region of cultural diversity and richness - in languages, religions, traditions, arts and cuisines. The countries of the Indian Ocean Rim vary considerably in terms of their areas, populations and levels of economic development.

After the British hegemony in the Indian Ocean ended, superpower rivalry in the region escalated, due to the strategic importance of the area. The common historical and geo-political experiences engendered a sense of shared identity among the states of the region. This, in turn, rekindled awareness about the centuries-old economic, social and cultural communities and traditions that exist all along the shores of the Indian Ocean. This sense of shared identity was further aroused after Nelson Mandela's visit to India in 1995, during which he had stated,

> "The natural urge of the facts of history and geography should broaden itself to include the concept of an Indian Ocean Rim for socio-economic co-operation and other peaceful endeavors. Recent changes in the international system demand that the countries of the Indian Ocean become a single platform."

This is the sentiment and rationale that underpinned the Indian Ocean Rim Initiative in March 1995, and the creation of the Indian Ocean Rim Association (then known as the Indian Ocean Rim Association for Regional Co-operation) two years later, in March 1997. IORA was formally launched at the first Ministerial Meeting in Mauritius on 6-7 March 1997. This meeting adopted the IORA Charter, and determined the administrative and procedural framework within which the organisation would develop. To promote the sustained growth and balanced development of the region and of the Member States, and to create common ground for regional economic co-operation, six priority areas were identified at the 11th Council of Ministers Meeting, in Bengaluru:

(i) Maritime Safety & Security,

(ii) Trade & Investment Facilitation,

(iii) Fisheries Management,

(iv) Disaster Risk Management,

(v) Academic, Science & Technology,

(vi) Tourism & Cultural Exchanges, and

(vii) Gender Empowerment

Today, IORA is a dynamic organization of 20 Member States and 6 Dialogue Partners, with an ever-growing momentum for mutually beneficial regional co-operation.

Appendix B

Charter of the Indian Ocean Rim Association (IORA)

Background

The Charter was adopted by the IOR Ministerial meeting held in Mauritius in March 1997 when the Indian Ocean Rim Association (IORA), formerly known as the Indian Ocean Rim Association for Regional Cooperation (IOR-ARC), was formally launched.

The Charter outlines the fundamental principles, objectives, areas of cooperation, and institutional and financial structures and arrangements of the Association. This was considered a historic decision of vital political importance to the Indian Ocean Rim countries as it formally launched the Association. It opens a new era of cooperation among Member States of the Association for their mutual benefit and for the welfare of their peoples.

The Charter declares that IORA seeks to build and expand understanding and mutually beneficial cooperation through a consensus-based, evolutionary and non-intrusive approach. In keeping with this spirit, there are no laws, binding contracts or rigid institutional structures.

Cooperation is based on the principles of sovereign equality, territorial integrity, political independence, non-interference in internal affairs, peaceful coexistence and mutual benefit.

Membership is open to all sovereign states of the Indian Ocean Rim willing to subscribe to the principles and objectives of the Charter. The IORA is firmly committed to the principle of open regionalism, as encouraged by the WTO.

All issues likely to generate controversy, create discord or impede regional cooperation are explicitly excluded from deliberations. Decisions, on all matters and issues and at all levels, are taken on the basis of consensus.

Cooperation within the Association is without prejudice to the rights and obligations of Member States within the framework of other economic and trade cooperation arrangements and will not apply automatically to

Member States of the Association. The Association does not seek to be a substitute for, but rather to reinforce, complement and be consistent with the bilateral and multilateral rights and obligations of Member States.

Within the framework of the Association, Member States will pursue measures to promote the achievement of its objectives, and will not take any action likely to hinder its objectives and activities.

The Charter was amended twice since 1997: in 2010 during the Council of Ministers' (COM) meeting in Yemen to revitalise the Association and in 2014 following the change of the name of the Association from "IOR-ARC" to "IORA".

The signature of the IORA Charter was proposed in 2014 in order to secure observer status in UN Specialised agencies. A formal signing ceremony was arranged at the COM in Perth, Australia, October 2014 and to append the signatures of representatives of Member States on the approved amended IORA Charter.

The IORA Charter is a less-than-treaty level document and therefore not legally binding.

Preamble

The Governments of Australia, People's Republic of Bangladesh, Union of the Comoros, Republic of India, Republic of Indonesia, Islamic Republic of Iran, Republic of Kenya, Republic of Madagascar, Federation of Malaysia, Republic of Mauritius, Republic of Mozambique, Sultanate of Oman, Republic of Seychelles, Republic of Singapore, Republic of South Africa, Democratic Socialist Republic of Sri Lanka, United Republic of Tanzania, Kingdom of Thailand, United Arab Emirates and Republic of Yemen:

CONSCIOUS of historical bonds created through millennia among the peoples of the Indian Ocean Rim and with a sense of recovery of history;

COGNIZANT of economic transformation and speed of change the world over which is propelled significantly by increased intensity in regional economic co-operation;

REALISING that the countries washed by the Indian Ocean in their diversity, offer vast opportunities to enhance economic interaction and co-operation over a wide spectrum to mutual benefit and in a spirit of equality;

CONVINCED that the Indian Ocean Rim, by virtue of past shared experience and geo-economic linkages among Member States, is poised for the creation of an effective Association and practical modalities of economic co-operation; and

CONSCIOUS of their responsibility to promote the welfare of their peoples by improving their standards of living and quality of life.

INTENDING the present Charter to replace the Charter of the Association as adopted in 1997 and amended in 2010;Australia, Bangladesh, India, Indonesia, Islamic Republic of Iran, Kenya, Madagascar, Malaysia, Mauritius, Mozambique, Sultanate of Oman, Singapore, South Africa, Sri Lanka, Tanzania, Thailand, United Arab Emirates and Yemen.

CONSIDERING that the 13th Council of Ministers in Perth, Australia, agreed to a new name of the Association as the "Indian Ocean Rim Association" (IORA);

Fundamental Principles

The Association will facilitate and promote economic co-operation, bringing together inter-alia representatives of Member States' governments, businesses and academia. In a spirit of multilateralism, the Association seeks to build and expand understanding and mutually beneficial co-operation through a consensus-based, evolutionary and non-intrusive approach. The Association will apply the following fundamental principles without qualification or exception to all Member States:-

(a) Co-operation within the framework of the Association will be based on respect for the principles of sovereign equality, territorial integrity, political independence, non-interference in internal affairs, peaceful co-existence and mutual benefit;

(b) The membership of the Association will be open to all sovereign States of the Indian Ocean Rim which subscribe to the principles and objectives of the Charter and are willing to undertake commitments under the Charter;

(c) Decisions on all matters and issues and at all levels will be taken on the basis of consensus;

(d) Bilateral and other issues likely to generate controversy and be an impediment to regional co-operation efforts will be excluded from deliberations;

(e) Co-operation within the Association is without prejudice to rights and obligations entered into by Member States within the framework of other economic and trade co-operation arrangements which will not automatically apply to Member States of the Association. It will not be a substitute for, but seeks to reinforce, be complementary to and consistent with their bilateral, plurilateral and multilateral obligations;

(f) A member-driven approach will be followed by Member States to achieve the goals and objectives of the Association;

(g) Promotion of principles of good governance by Member States will enable smooth implementation of programmes.

Objectives

(a) To promote the sustained growth and balanced development of the region and of the Member States, and to create common ground for regional economic co-operation;

(b) To focus on those areas of economic co-operation which provide maximum opportunities to develop shared interests and reap mutual benefits. Towards this end, to formulate and implement projects for economic co-operation relating to trade facilitation and liberalization, promotion of foreign investment, scientific and technological exchanges, tourism, movement of natural persons and service providers on a non-discriminatory basis; and the development of infrastructure and human resources inter-alia poverty alleviation,promotion of maritime transport and related matters, cooperation in the fields of fisheries trade, research and management, aquaculture, education and training, energy, IT, health, protection of the environment, agriculture, disaster management.

(c) To seek to reinvigorate the Association by progressing the prioritised agenda decided upon at the Council of Ministers› meeting in Bengaluru in November 2011. That meeting gave a focused direction towards formulation of a dynamic road map of cooperation, in consonance with the growing global emphasis on the unique geo-strategic primacy of the Indian Ocean rim. The priority areas are: (i) Maritime Safety and Security; (ii) Trade and Investment Facilitation; (iii) Fisheries Management; (iv) Disaster Risk Management; (v) Academic, Science & Technology Cooperation; and (vi) Tourism and Cultural Exchanges;

(d) To explore all possibilities and avenues for trade liberalisation, to remove impediments to, and lower barriers towards, freer and enhanced flow of goods, services, investment, and technology within the region;

(e) To encourage close interaction of trade and industry, academic institutions, scholars and the peoples of the Member States without any discrimination among Member States and without prejudice to obligations under other regional economic and trade co-operation arrangements;

(f) To strengthen co-operation and dialogue among Member States in international fora on global economic issues, and where desirable to develop shared strategies and take common positions in the international fora on issues of mutual interest; and

(g) To promote co-operation in development of human resources, particularly through closer linkages among training institutions, universities and other specialised institutions of the Member States.

Appendix C

Background Note

Meeting of Experts on Maritime Safety and Security

Indian Ocean Rim Association (IORA) formerly known as Indian Ocean Rim Association for Regional Cooperation (IOR-ARC) currently represents a grouping of 20 countries (Australia, Bangladesh, Comoros, India, Indonesia, Iran, Kenya, Malaysia, Madagascar, Mauritius, Mozambique, Oman, Seychelles, Singapore, South Africa, Sri Lanka, Tanzania, Thailand, UAE and Yemen) whose shores are washed by the Indian ocean and collectively aim at enhancing economic cooperation for sustained development and balanced economic growth of its members. It has 6 Dialogue Partners: China, Egypt, France, Japan, UK and USA. There are two observers: Indian Ocean Tourism Organisation (IOTO) and Indian Ocean Research Group (IORG). The Name IORA was adopted in November 2013 in Perth, Australia during the 13th meeting of Foreign Ministers.

At the 11th Council of Ministers (COM) meeting in Bengaluru, India in November 2011, six priority areas were identified on the basis of an Indian proposal to focus cooperation amongst member states of IORA in the years to come. One of the areas so identified was Maritime Safety and Security.

During the deliberations of the 15th bi-annual Committee of Senior Officials (CSOs) meeting in Mauritius on 28-29 May 2015, it was decided that the recommendations which have been made during the various events organised on the theme of Maritime Safety and Security be thoroughly examined in much greater detail by a meeting of experts on the subject, which is the aim of this meeting.

Recommendations

A series of recommendations were made in the past events regarding maritime safety and security. These recommendations were first considered at the CSO in Perth in October 2014. The IORA Secretariat summarised the recommendations requiring further consideration or action as follows:

(a) The appointment of National Focal Points for Maritime Security and consideration for the establishment of a Maritime Security Working Group/Core Group.

(b) To consider the inclusion of more Dialogue Partner States, such as South Korea (as well as Russia, Germany and New Zealand), amongst others, and to increase the roles of the existing Dialogue Partners.

(c) The establishment of an "eminent persons group" to foster modalities for multilateral security cooperation and for the development of a coordinated regional maritime security.

(d) IORAG to establish a "study group" to conduct studies to identify strategic interest areas in security/economic/investment/ environmental/maritime issues among IORA Member States (including capacity building and training programmes).

(e) Considering the establishment of an IORA Legal Group of Experts that could also conduct regional training and to develop a legal framework for maritime security in the Indian Ocean Region (the ratification of applicable international legal conventions on maritime security and creating a system for the resolution of disputes among IORA Member States).

(f) During the last of these events – the Blue Economy workshop in South Africa - the recommendations included:

   (i) Establishing a platform for cooperation to reduce transnational crime.

   (ii) Establishment of a common contact point and regional mechanism for sharing information.

   (iii) Establishment of a database of existing information.

   (iv) Establishment of a comprehensive Maritime Plan in relation to seawater quantity and quality.

   (v) Establishment of Regional Centres to strengthen cooperation.

The outcome of this Experts' meeting would then be carried forward to the 16th CSOs meeting of the IORA.

Appendix D

Conference Programme

Day One (Tuesday, 13 October 2015)

0900-0930h	**Registration and Tea**
0930-1000h	**Inaugural Session**

Welcome Address: Dr. Vijay Sakhuja, Director, National Maritime Foundation

Keynote Address: Ms. Sujata Mehta, Secretary (M & ER), Ministry of External Affairs

1000-1130h	**Session I: Maritime Safety and Security: Regional Challenges**

Chair: RAdm. Monty Khanna
Naval War College, India

Speakers: Mr. Swee Lean Collin Koh

S. Rajaratnam School of International Studies, Singapore

Capt. Martin A. Sebastian
Royal Malaysian Navy (R), Malaysia

Cdr. (Navy) Randrianantenaina Jean Edmond, Malagasy Naval Forces Command, Madagascar

Ms. Bhagya Senaratne

General Sir John Kotelawala, Defence University, Sri Lanka

1130-1200h	**Tea**

1200-1315h	**Session II: Cooperative Organisational Structures in the IOR**
Chair:	Prof. KS Nathan, Malaysian Institute of Defence & Security (MIDAS), Malaysia
Speakers:	Prof. GVC Naidu, Jawaharlal Nehru University, India
	Mr. Francis Kornegay,
	Institute for Global Dialogue-University of South Africa, South Africa
	Ms. Sumathy Permal, Centre for Straits of Malacca, Malaysia
1315-1415h	**Lunch**
1415-1545h	**Session III: Inclusive Approach to Maritime Safety and Security**
Chair:	RAdm. Ranaivoseheno Louis Antoine de Padoue, Ministry of National Defense, Madagascar
Speakers:	Mr. Thomas Benjamin Daniel, Institute of Strategic and International Studies (ISIS), Malaysia
	Mr. Boetse Able Ramahlo, South African Maritime Safety Agency, South Africa **(In Lieu of Cdr Tsietsi Mokhele)**

Day Two (Wednesday, 14 October 2015)

0830-0900h	**Tea**

0900-1030h	**Session IV: Legal Frameworks and Maritime Security**
Chair:	Mrs. Nancy Wakarima Karigithu, Former DG, Kenya Maritime Authority (KMA), Kenya
Speakers:	Prof. Stuart Bruce Kaye, University of Wollongong, Australia **(by Video Presentation)**
	Prof. Paul Musili Wambua, University of Nairobi School of Law, Kenya
	Capt. Somjade Kongrawd, Royal Thai Navy, Thailand
	Mr. Jacques Belle, Ministry of Foreign Affairs & CGPCS Secretariat, Seychelles
1030-1100h	**Tea**
1100-1230h	**Session V: Capability Building and Capacity Optimization**
Chair:	Amb. Ahmed Salem Saleh Al-Wahishi, Yemeni International Affairs' Center (YIAC), Yemen
Speakers:	Dr Sinderpal Singh, Institute of South Asian Studies, National University of Singapore
	Cmde AJ Singh (Retd.) Indian Maritime Foundation, India
1230-1315h	**Concluding Session**
	Presentation of findings by Session Chairs and Summing up

Closing Address: Mr. Alok Amitabh Dimri (Director, M & ER Division)

Vote of Thanks: Director, NMF

1315-1430h **Lunch**

Contributors

Mr. Swee Lean Collin Koh
Associate Research Fellow
S. Rajaratnam School of International Studies, Singapore

Mr. Swee Lean Collin Koh is an associate research fellow at the Maritime Security Programme of the Institute of Defence and Strategic Studies, a constituent unit of the S. Rajaratnam School of International Studies (RSIS) based in Nanyang Technological University, Singapore. His research interest covers naval affairs in the Indo-Pacific region, primarily focused on Southeast Asia. In that regard, Collin is keen on the study of naval technologies, offence-defence theory, naval arms control and non-provocative defence. He has also taught various courses since July 2010 at the Singapore Armed Forces Training Institute. His work appears in a number of policy magazines and peer-reviewed academic journals such as *India Review, Naval War College Review, The Diplomat* and *The National Interest*, and he has also authored chapters in edited volumes. In addition to research and teaching work, Collin contributes his perspectives to both local and international media.

Ms. Bhagya Senaratne
Lecturer
General Sir John Kotelawala Defence University, Sri Lanka

Ms. Bhagya Senaratne completed her Master of Arts in International Relations from the University of Colombo and her Bachelor of Arts from the University of Colombo. She has a Diploma in International Relations from the Bandaranaike Centre for International Studies (BCIS) and a Diploma in World Affairs & Professional Diplomacy from the Bandaranaike International Diplomatic Training Institute (BIDT).

Ms.Senaratne contributes extensively to local publications, and recently presented a research paper on "*Sri Lanka's Strategic Relevance in the*

South Asian Region: An Analysis of India's Indian Ocean Strategy and China's Maritime Silk Route Initiative" at the 8th International Research Conference of General Sir John Kotelawala Defence University. Among other areas, she researches on Public Diplomacy, Strategic Communication, Foreign Policy, Geopolitics and Sri Lanka's role in the Indian Ocean Region.

Prof. GVC Naidu
Centre for Indo-Pacific Studies
Jawaharlal Nehru University, India

G V C Naidu is Professor in the Centre for Indo-Pacific Studies, Jawaharlal Nehru University, New Delhi. His research interests include the Indian Ocean, the Indian Navy and East Asian maritime issues. His visiting appointments/professorships include Research Fellow at the Institute of Southeast Asian Studies, Singapore; Japan Foundation Visiting Professor at the Daito Bunka University, Japan; Visiting Fellow at the East-West Center, Honolulu; Visiting Fellow at the Japan Institute of International Affairs, Visiting Professor at Gakushuin University, Tokyo, and National Chengchi University, Taipei, etc.

He has to his credit five books, five monographs on various issues and a large number of articles, chapters in books, and research papers published in India and abroad. His most recent publications include two books on *Building Confidence in East Asia: Maritime Conflicts, Interdependence and Asian Identity Thinking* (Palgrave, 2015) (edited with Kazuhiko Togo) and *India and China in the Emerging Dynamics of East Asia* (Springer 2015) (edited with Mumin Chen).

Mr. Francis Kornegay
Senior Research Associate
Institute for Global Dialogue-University of South Africa, South Africa

Mr. Francis Kornegay is Senior Research Associate at the Institute for Global Dialogue-University of South Africa and former Global Fellow at The Wilson Centre in Washington, D.C. In 2014, he organized the first international symposium on Indian Ocean-South Atlantic maritime issues relating to South and Southern African interests. Kornegay led the first South African delegation to the 3rd BRICS think-tank symposium in Beijing in 2011, co-led the delegation to the 4th symposium in India. He has a BA in Political Science from the University of Michigan; MA in African Studies from Howard University and Masters in International Public Policy from the School of Advanced International Studies. As a fellow at the New Delhi based Observer Research Foundation in 2011, he produced an occasional paper on the Indian Ocean and the IBSA-BRICS equation.

Mr. Thomas Benjamin Daniel
Analyst
Institute of Strategic and International Studies (ISIS), Malaysia

Mr. Thomas Benjamin Daniel is an Analyst in the Foreign Policy and Security Studies Programme of ISIS Malaysia. His interests include security challenges and big power competition in ASEAN, as well as the relationship between ASEAN and regional powers. He obtained his Master of Arts in International Studies from the University of Nottingham (Malaysia) where he graduated with distinction, completing a dissertation that assessed Malaysia's responses to China in the South China Sea dispute through the balance of threat approach. He also holds a BA in Communication and Media Management, and a BA Honors in Communication, Media & Culture from the University of South Australia.

Captain Martin A. Sebastian
Royal Malaysian Navy (R)
Fellow, Centre Head, Maritime Security and Diplomacy
Maritime Institute of Malaysia (MIMA), Malaysia

Captain Martin A. Sebastian, Royal Malaysian Navy (R), joined MIMA in Nov 2011 as Fellow and Centre Head of the Centre for Maritime Security and Diplomacy. Prior to joining MIMA, Capt. Martin completed three years of Secondment with the Department of Peacekeeping Operations (DPKO), United Nations Headquarters, New York. He served in the Office of Military Affairs (OMA) as a Strategic Planner in the Military Planning Service (MPS). Capt. Martin is credited for leading a team in the drafting of a UN Policy for Maritime and Riverine Operations in Peacekeeping.

He is country representative in the Council for Security Cooperation in the Asia Pacific (CSCAP) and Indian Ocean Rim Association (IORA) Maritime Security Study Group. He has presented in the ASEAN Regional Forum Inter- Sessional Meeting on Maritime Security (ARF – ISM MS), ASEAN Defence Ministers Plus Expert Working Group (ADMM Plus EWG), ASEAN Maritime Forum (AMF) and the annual Workshop on Managing Potential Conflicts in the South China Sea.

Prof. Stuart Kaye
Australian National Centre for Ocean Resources and Security
University of Wollongong, Australia

Prof. Stuart Kaye is Director and Professor of Law at the Australian National Centre for Ocean Resources and Security at the University of Wollongong. Prior to this appointment, he was Dean and Winthrop Professor of Law at the University of Western Australia. He also previously held a Chair in Law at the University of Melbourne and was Dean of Law at the University of Wollongong between 2002 and 2006. He holds degrees in arts and law from the University of Sydney, and a doctorate in law from Dalhousie University. He has written around 100 books, chapters and articles, principally in international law. He was chair of the Australian International Humanitarian Law Committee from 2003 to 2009. He is a Fellow of the Royal Geographical Society and the Australian Academy of Law. He holds the rank of Commander in the Royal Australian Navy Reserve, principally providing advice in respect of operations and international law.

Captain Somjade Kongrawd
Royal Thai Navy (RTN), Thailand

Captain SomjadeKongrawd is the Director Military Legislation and Foreign Affairs Division, Office of the Judge Advocate General, Royal Thai Navy (RTN), Operational Legal Officer, at Naval Operational Centre and Thai Maritime Enforcement Coordinating Centre, and Judge in Appeal Military Court. Previously, he has held positions like the Staff Judge Advocate General (SJA), Naval Supply Department, SJA, Royal Thai Fleet (1986), Instructor, Naval Warfare and Military Operations Division, Institute of Advanced Naval Studies for Humanitarian Law/LOAC/Law of War and Law of the Sea at Naval War College and Naval Staff College .

He holds a Bachelor of Law, Ramkamhaeng University, Thailand, Master of Law (Public Law), Thammasat University, Master of Art (Maritime Policy), University of Wollongong, Australia. He has written extensively on Thailand and Cambodia Maritime Dispute: Peaceful Settlement, The implementation of Thai Domestic Law to the UNCLOS. His research interests include Maritime Law and the influence on Thailand's Sea Powers.

Commodore Anil Jai Singh (Retd)
Vice-President
Indian Maritime Foundation (New Delhi Branch), India

Commodore Anil Jai Singh is the Vice President and heads the Delhi branch of the Indian Maritime Foundation. He took early retirement from the Navy in March 2011 after serving for three decades. A submariner and ASW specialist, he commanded four submarines and a Fleet ship. His varied shore appointments included tenures in the Directorates of Submarine Acquisition and Naval Plans at Naval Headquarters and his last appointment was as the Deputy Assistant Chief (Maritime) in the Perspective Planning and Force Development branch of the Integrated Defence Staff in the MoD. He also served as the Defence and Naval Adviser at the Indian High Commission in London.

A post-graduate in Defence and Strategic Studies, he is an alumnus of the National Defence Academy, the Defence Services Staff College and the Naval War College and has also been a Directing Staff at the College. He takes keen interest in matters maritime and writes and speaks on the subject at various fora in India and abroad.

Captain (Dr.) Gurpreet Singh Khurana
Executive Director
National Maritime Foundation

Captain Gurpreet Singh Khurana is a serving Indian Navy officer with 27 years of commissioned service, and a PhD in Defence Studies. A missile specialist and ship's diver, he has participated in all major naval operations since IPKF operations (1987–90) and has held the command of two warships, including the commissioning command of a Fast Attack Craft at the Andaman and Nicobar Command (2002).

During his Research Fellowship at the IDSA (2003–8), he authored the book titled '*Maritime Forces in Pursuit of National Security*' (2008). He was commended by the Chief of Indian Navy for reviewing and editing the *Indian Maritime Doctrine*, 2009 (INBR-8). He also compiled the Navy's *Handbook on the Law of Maritime Operations*, 2013 (INBR-1652) in three volumes. His second book titled '*Porthole: Geopolitical, Strategic and Maritime Terms and Concepts*' (2015) is being published.

He represents India at the Search and Rescue (SAR) Working Group of the *Council for Security Cooperation in the Asia-Pacific* (CSCAP). He is currently the Executive Director at the *National Maritime Foundation* (NMF), New Delhi.

Index